HOMOGENIZING RELIGION

A Metaphilosophy for 1,000 years!

Herbert Siegel

Cover art by Harriet Slaughter
Early manuscript scan by Steven Pinderb Schmidt
Manuscript editing by Fredda Gordon
Interior Design by Josh Laluna

Author's website: www.herbsiegel.org

Order this book online at www.trafford.com
or email orders@trafford.com

Most Trafford titles are also available at major online book retailers.

Print information available on the last page.

ISBN: 978-1-6987-1256-7 (hc)
ISBN: 978-1-6987-1255-0 (e)

Library of Congress Control Number: 2022914491

Trafford rev. 11/28/2022

 www.trafford.com
North America & international
toll-free: 844-688-6899 (USA & Canada)
fax: 812 355 4082

"The voice in my dreams may not be real, but it has good ideas."

Dedicated to:

Harriet Frances Slaughter of Texas, BA, MFA

A direct descendant of Martha Washington

"Tell me a story about the Bronx!"

CONTENTS

PART I: IT'S HAPPENING NOW
pp. 7-138

The Ambassadors

Religionists

The Media

Academia

Peer Conferences

An Episode

The Next Morning

The Galactic Dream

Dreams

Cosmic Telepathy

Religious Debates That Ensue

Catholicism

Earth Cables

Islamism

A Dream Coda for Islamists

Judaic Kabbalists

The Fabulist

Dream Coda for Kabbalists

Christianity

Dream Coda for Christians

Buddhism

Dream Coda for Buddhists

PART II: A CENTURY LATER

pp. 139-232

PART III: FIVE HUNDRED YEARS LATER
pp. 233-276

What the World Looks Like
Turning Points
The World Order
The Unknown Unknowns
A Word about Aliennus
The Most Compelling Dream in Five Hundred Years
The Next Morning
A Proclamation Humanus for AD 2649
For People of the Earth

PART IV: ONE THOUSAND YEARS LATER
pp. 277-307

The New Millennium
Mission Accomplished
Dreamcast 1—Looking Back
Questions and Answers
Terra Incognito
A Novel Society for the Third Millenmium
Everyday Life in AD 3014
The Loss of Certainty
Magic Economics
The New Apotheosis: Are We Trapped
by History, or Is History Trapped by Us?
Omnicide
The Surprise

INTRODUCTION

Send spaceships into the cosmos with return-address nameplates to search for extraterrestrial life and perhaps find cabbages growing somewhere or a planet full of Einsteins—these are astronomical crapshoots. They are mankind's dream of communing with another species. We tried for millennia but still lack dialogue with other earthbound animals, microorganisms, or any of the 4,200 religious deities we imagined. There are only one-way discourses. What is it we are up against? This is a story of what happened before, during, and after we experienced omnicide.

By mathematically modeling an individual's chance of existence and finding the odds are 300,000,000:13 against it, going back only three generations, does humanity result from a grand plan or an accident? Are we just metaphors in a hologram of the string theory, and if so, for what or whom? And how would we recognize the answer if there was one? The obtuse side of reality is fantasy. We possess an imagination enhanced by a proclivity for simultaneous insights into quantum physics and gigantism. We can imagine penetrating these spectrums and all degrees in between with equations to prove a hypothesis that satisfies us or pays homage to a belief we can't cogently explain—all to prove human domination over all things living and innate. Of course, our cognition shifts back and forth as we strive to become legends in our own minds.

Despite archiving a millennium of futile efforts for use by our descendants, what remains unknown to us far exceeds the sum of the knowledge we possess at any given time. The black holes of the unknowable are perceived either as a complexity of the big bang, a limitation on mankind's ability to think, or a religious mystique of the supernatural, depending on our individual psychological profile. Ever since Copernicus discovered that Earth was not the center of the universe, and Darwin found that mankind was another evolution of an animal uniquely ruled by unconscious desires and furies, any attempt to define the great disparity between galactic knowledge and mankind is foredoomed.

A COSMIC HOROLOGY

Perceived encounters between foreign life-forms and people formed the basis for every anomaly experienced on Earth during the first and second millennium. Ancient hypotheses were founded on patterns of art, engineering, and periods of greater cognition, prophesies and cave drawings, pyramids of Egypt, Stonehenge, the theory of relativity, World War I and II, and nuclear tests. Numerous motives were imagined for human abduction for purposes of genital examinations, altering the human genome, survival of an alien race, and destruction of Earth, yet no scientific evidence was ever discovered to justify these hysterics, eyewitness accounts notwithstanding. Proving the axiom that little knowledge is a dangerous thing, the theory of quantum entanglement, also known as the entropy of entanglement, arose during the second millennium. It posited our universe as two-dimensional although we see it as three-dimensional, much like a hologram. This mind-twisting notion proposed that gravity evident in the space-time quadrant comports with quantum fields as small as an atom designed (by aliens) to deliberately distort our view of the cosmos! This was soon followed by the blue skies theory, a.k.a. research without a clear goal, which entertained proposals to radically change the way people think about anything and everything.

Then there were those whose mindsets changed when facts conflicted with their beliefs, and they acted upon what they concluded was righteous. They were motivated by piety and reverence to the exclusion of scientifically proven facts. It was cases of cognition altered by how they thought the world should function, as though sacred values in the supernatural were immune to facts of life. Magnificently constructed temples were often thought of as portals to heaven though built by mankind for meditating. These were not dumb people who strained reasoning to enhance morality rather than face facts. Others pursued a passion for mysticism to corral the universe down to a singular belief. Almost everything inexplicable became a gateway to panocracy. The sea of anomalies flowed like waves of electromagnetic energy, and the planet glowed with as many extraterrestrial thoughts as light, radio, and microwaves. It was as though the earth itself was thinking!

One such theory came from a Jesuit priest trained as a scientist and a religious mystic—oxymora were not rare. He viewed the world as evolving from a dead planet to one of mindless biological life, ever certain vegetation would lead to a universal consciousness that was housed in a thinking sphere, or knowledge sphere, circling above the biosphere, accessible to evolving matter. The closest we came to realizing it, in the second millennium, was trading mindless network TV in exchange for absorbing scientific information over the internet. Of course, it soon changed into another mindless social forum.

GLOSSARY

An Epitome for 1,000 Years

Aliennus	A prophetic spirit from Paraspermya and the protagonist
alkaline hydrolysis	A chemical process for body disposal
amplituhedron	A geometric particle measure
apotheosis	Developing a higher state of mind
AU	Astronomical unit; one astronomical unit equals the distance between the earth and the sun
bibliophilic didactus	Devotion to book learning
cobots	Autonomous robots
consilato synod	Committee meeting
civilment	A society that equally values every type of contribution
DIF	Decisions dictated by the digitally induced logic of artificial intelligence
digital recombinant	Designer genes
dreamcast	A dream that can be called upon like a podcast
episteme	A philosophical understanding
ecomiums	Understanding economic systems
eschatological	Final destination of the human soul
fulminology	Harnessing lightning
ganglia	Relay stations between neurons
humanus	Philosophy of fulfillment
homeotherms	Warm-blooded creatures

heterodox	Non-conformers
Kabbalah	Jewish mysticism
Kardashev scale	Measurement of technological achievement
metaphysical	Abstractions of the human mind
mensa	Genius IQ society
Mahabharata	The epic Hindu spirituality
Maecenas	Patron of the arts
natrium	Sodium additive
noosphere	Sense of consciousness
omnicide	Human destruction
panocracy	Religions ruling the universe
Paraspermya	A fictionalized swarm of primary knowledge forever streaming among the cosmos
polyglot	Multilingual
Rig Veda	Hindi hymns
string theory	One-dimensional particle theory for quantum gravity
syncretism	An amalgamation of religions
terra incognita	Land, but nothing more
UFOlogy	UFO pseudoscience
Watson	A colloquial for the first supercomputer

PART I

IT'S HAPPENING NOW

THE AMBASSADORS

RELIGIONISTS

Pope Luke II awoke startled from a restless night the day after his ascension to the papacy by unanimous vote of the conclave of fasting cardinals who handed him a flue opener for the escaping column of white smoke. The humble bishop immediately took the papal name of one of Christ's lesser disciples. After blessing the faithful minions gathered in Vatican Square, he broke the fast with his brethren in the state dining hall of the Vatican with attendees including Cardinals Arevedecchi, head of the Vatican Bank, who was seated to his immediate right; Luigi Legalo, an expert in canonical and pedophilic law, who sat to his left; the eminent Bwana Straightpath of South Africa, a fundamentalist and church archivist; and seven retired and forty other Roman Catholic princes. Seated at the annexed table (a.k.a. the kids' table) were Msgr. John Stewart, chief of staff and first assistant to the pope, and an assortment of other bishops and monks. No women were present.

The Inaugural Menu

*Red wine with rice crackers in
a common golden chalice
(for the devotion to the Christ)
Bagels, lox, and cream cheese
(to pay homage to Jewish ancestry)
Caesar salad
(to honor the Vatican in Rome)
St. Peter's fish with angel hair pasta
(to pay homage to Catholic ancestry)
Assorted Italian figs and fruits
(fresh from the corner market)
Cognac and Cuban cigars
(a holy pairing)*

A roundtable discussion followed, wherein Cardinal Arevedecchi reported on the solvency of the Vatican Bank. As expected, its profit-making holdings were extremely liquid, as was its investment portfolio of 1 trillion euros. The annual stipend to each prince of the church for their personal use continued uninterrupted for over a thousand years. Worldwide, the church's outlier assets were less stable, principally due to heavy reserves for legal fees and settlements of pedophilic litigation when approved by Cardinal Legalo. It was agreed that consequent cash shortfalls were offset by reducing childhood education programs and aid to the poor or indigent rather than raid the personal funds forthcoming from the Vatican.

The archivist and fundamentalist Cardinal Straightpath of South Africa reported lay membership and contributions were uniformly declining throughout the world despite aggressive proselytizing for right-to-life, antigay, and misogynist church practices. He appeared genuinely confused. Overall, the financial condition of the Roman Catholic Church as a whole was precarious. This was principally due to millennia of escalating religious skirmishes, wars, and modern molestation scandals—the resolution of which often required large legal outlays and remedial compensation to victims. After this report, the breakfast was concluded.

The next order of business for the newly elected holy father was to place a conference call to his five favorite religious CEOs, hoping to get them to agree to a secret meeting to discuss the obstacles to religious peace—a consilato synod. His contemporaries for this call included the supreme mullah of Islam, the chief rabbi of Jerusalem, the bishop of Canterbury, the Dalai Lama, and the Russian Orthodox pope.

Ensconced alone in the grandiose office of the pontiff, he placed the conference call himself to each of their unpublished phone numbers, which he was privy to from his old friends, now his peers; and as he awaited the connections, he paced the spacious quarters while convincing himself that somewhere between a monastic cell and these grandiose quarters was a working office where he would be comfortable. Afterward, he looked into the modestly furnished Santa Marta guesthouse as his permanent office and residence.

While expecting a shrill ringing at any moment, he was, nonetheless, taken aback when he heard the peeling of bells as if coming from a steeple—*ding, dong, ding, dong.* It was indeed his phone ringing, modified long ago by Pius V to remind himself that whoever speaks here does so for the entire church. The conference call successfully gathered the participants on the line despite interrupting their activities, whether it was another meeting, prayer, luncheon, or sleep.

His peers stood ready to take his call.

Luke's sense of euphoria when the idea to call first struck was now distilled into a slight trepidation. Silently he prayed none would be offended by his usurping upon their daily routine. He carefully lifted the gilded ceramic receiver revered by some of his predecessors while he spoke, "God bless you all for forgiving my abruptness, but I felt compelled to comport with you on this first day of my papacy because I need your help."

"Abrupt, *geschmut*, Luke, alas *iss forgessen*, and I wish you a mazel tov," said Moise, an old colleague and now chief rabbi of Jerusalem.

"Thank you, Moise, my dear friend. It will take some time for me to get my sea legs here at St. Peter's, and before they rope me in completely, I want to get our holy half dozen together for a private session, and don't worry, I'll pick up the tab this time," Luke laughingly said in broken Yiddish.

The fifteenth Dalai Lama, Patriarch Krill of the Russian Orthodox Church, and the supreme mullah—known amongst themselves as Abbruzu, Sabastian, and AliBaba, respectively—talked on top of one another.

"I'll bring the yak dish," said Abbruzu while Sabastian said, "I got the borscht!"

"I'll take care of the hookah and couscous," said AliBaba in broken English as they all cheered.

The bishop of Canterbury, an Elizabethan by birthright, hanging back to take in the banter among his religious peers and longtime friends, sneeringly decided on a more formal greeting to Luke. Aside from being an elder, he was a doctrinaire, and although he had a caring persona, he was often perceived as distant or shy. He found it difficult to let his hair down, so to speak, preferring to project a typical image of an Anglican pastor with a steel rod spine. He spoke in subdued tones with superb diction, "First of all, Luke, I want to congratulate and bless you as a fellow Christian and assure you of my devotion to your success, and bless my dear friends and peers for whom I pray every day. Nothing pleases me more than to join with you for a discussion. What is on your mind, Luke?"

Luke responded, "Thank you, all. I know you are as concerned as I about the escalating violence perpetrated in the name of religion. I ask you to join me in a consilato synod of peace to seek divine guidance to end this brutal side of religion. Together we can arrive at a pinnacle to lead our flocks in a universal prayer of petition so the Lord can shine his countenance upon humanity and grant us peace from the unintended consequences of our religious beliefs. Our world needs this now more than ever before."

"Amen" was said in unison. They agreed to meet at a date and time to be decided.

THE MEDIA

Meanwhile, in the media world, international TV networks were agreeing to simulcast a debate among notable biblical scholars of major religions at a different time and place—a bibliophilic didactus.

Rather than label a public interest discussion about religion as a disputation, reformation, or proselytization, the major world TV networks opted for an informal roundtable discourse. Silvio Bertolani, the scion of the Italy news and entertainment network Ungatz, argued to narrow participation to converts only in order to titillate paying sponsors while enticing an educated and overindulgent consumer audience. Conrad White of BBC emphasized the need for formal and fixed rules of engagement. Manny Bloomberg of CNN sought to declare winners and losers at the end, as in a prizefight. The Australians, represented by Robert Murdoch of Fox, insisted on the option to polemically revise the tape before airing it to add innuendo and sensationalism to it. The attempted commercialization of this serious undertaking soon gave way to airing the views of biblical scholars for world peace. Lastly, Petro Poroshenko of Investia invited China, Japan, Africa, and India to join, at a time and place to be decided, with a program structure to be agreed upon.

ACADEMIA

Elsewhere, deans of academia shared their troubled but conforming diversion from mentoring students to assuaging donors and alumni on the internet while agreeing to a much-needed forum on new age apps, to discuss the urgent need for a new look at undergraduate liberal education, and figure out how to continue the search for world peace. For this, they unanimously agreed to empanel the great philosophers of our time, a philosophia moralis. The idea arose from the editorial board of *Who's Who in Academia*, the chronicle of college deans that first noticed a radical change in their bios by ranking fundraising, alumni relations, outside consultancies, and technical job placements as best educational practices and de-emphasizing student guidance, humanities, and management as meaningful achievements. Their interest in the student body was to graduate them with technical and business skills needed for corporate profiteering with little or no liberal and cultural education, which is so essential for society to function peacefully.

The changing curricula and new ethics dissipated the integrity of student mentoring to be replaced by modified lesson plans to assuage important alumni and other donors who prided themselves as university trustees of influence in graduating a workforce of football fanatics at the expense of providing coed students a well-rounded liberal education despite faculty protesters. Mollifying these outliers became a full-time endeavor for college deans, all of whom were in desperate need of guidance to restore their role as gateways to higher human standards. It was left to the editors of *Who's Who* to plan a webinar for fifty thousand college deans with a panel of world-renowned philosophers to redefine their roles in higher education.

PEER CONFERENCES

International conferences that convened to disseminate peer data among members seemingly took a renewed sense of urgency. It was as though almost everybody experienced skittishness and unexplained angst. Symposiums and conferences previously scheduled were to be held earlier, and future ones were hastily arranged. An inexplicable sense of urgency seemed to infect everyone. Scientists, politicians, diplomats, the military, pollsters, statisticians, and medical and psychological professionals clamored for thoughtful interchanges to satisfy their thirst for knowledge to relieve these perceived behavioral anomalies. Hastily convened peer groups evolved to denominate their specialty and ad hoc authority to investigate and opine to the quizzical public. These, among other international forums, included an international scientia technique, a supreme military alliance, the assembly of industry and trades, the proletariat polity, and a council on human longevity.

News headlines and live TV captured this worldwide restlessness by proclaiming the climate was ripe for an episteme. Sidewalk preachers predicted a second coming or dreamed of the world's end. Something was in the wind.

AN EPISODE

THE NEXT MORNING

The earth's sixty-ninth rotation of AD 2014 was atypical compared to the eternal spin of 365 axial turns since time immemorial to travel once around the sun. On this particular day's spin, however, an episodic identical dream was experienced during every person's sleep.

Newscaster: Breaking news! Associated Press, BBC, Al Jazeera, Bloomberg, and other major news agencies reported unusual activity on the International Space Station yesterday when each of the six astronauts experienced identical dreams during their sleep cycles. This was revealed in transmitted recordings of conversations while performing their spaceship duties. Part of the discussion follows:

Commander Sanat Ercan [upon resuming her duties after sleeping]: Hi, everyone, I am back on station and feeling exuberant after a great sleep and an incredible dream.

Lt. Akbaba Lepage: Good morning, Sanat, I hope I am as lucky as you as I am about to begin my sleep cycle.

Sanat Ercan: I hope so, Aki, and am anxious for your critique when you awake.

Sergeant Prim Venkatesman [and Sergeant Geraldine Bellini]:

Sanat, Aki, we were just discussing the incredible dreams we both experienced today while in our sleep stations and learned they were identical except it was in our native languages. Sanat, tell us about your dream, please. This is getting spooky.

Sanat Ercan: Wow, you two had the same dream on the same subjects on the same day, and was it like mine? My dream was about [*garbled transmission*]. Does that sound familiar to either of you?

Sergeant Prim Venkatesman: Holy smoke, we all had the same dream about the same thing on the same day in three different languages! What is happening up here?

Sanat Ercan: It's weird, I agree, but let's wait until Aki awakes before I officially log this in and report back to headquarters. They will think we hallucinated.

Sergeant Geraldine Bellini: We agree to wait for Aki. Of course, she now knows about what we experienced since she hasn't slept yet, but her native language differs from any of ours. That levels the playing field [*silence*].

On Earth, interviews were conducted worldwide and revealed identical dream episodes were experienced by everyone, each in their mother tongue, on the same day of their circadian sleep cycle, a heretofore unheard-of phenomenon! "No comment" was offered by NASA, NSA, the National Academy of Sciences, the Austrian Psychiatric Association, UN, and any other governmental and professional organizations that were interviewed. Worldwide rumors were rampant and were soon cited as confirmation of a mysterious dream event that was replicated 3 billion times and simultaneously translated in six thousand languages. Instant polls determined the remaining 4 billion people on the planet who were asleep when the first poll was taken also had an identical dream. Every TV viewer in each country was treated to an array of expert talking heads who speculated the event was predictable or natural given the evolution of the human species. Attempted explanations went from extreme stress, a mass phobia, metaphysical epiphany, thought control platforms launched by China, and hacking by Cuba to declarations of proof that C. Jung was right to declare dreams as part of the universal consciousness, and that S. Freud was wrong to describe dreams as mind clearing filters for daily detritus. Notions of mass hypnotism and extraterrestrial aliens were also mentioned. Fire and brimstone preachers and sidewalk sages throughout the world all claimed exclusive contact with their god of choice.

The good news was a noticeable and palpable reduction in extreme stress, as new ideas permeated individual energy levels to inspire an eagerness for personal and global peace. Daily tasks were undertaken with vigor and bounce-in-the-step enthusiasm and inner sanguine. Journeys to eradicate major causes of anxiety were underway with a rare confluence of mind-bending acts that would change society forever.

THE GALACTIC DREAM

DREAMS

Dreams are inherently private imaginings, the assemblage of which presents, at the same instant, a series of images with no logical connection to reality. They can produce a starting point for an abundance of contagious suggestions, excite emotions, or hallucinations that appear so authentic as to equalize learned people with ignoramuses. Such are the mechanisms of a dream. The audacity of our imagination when awake is insignificant when compared with the temerity of a dream. Yet when we are awakened and recall our dreams, we cease to believe we were duped by them and momentarily enter a metacognitive state to assemble their complexity to the reality of wakefulness. Undoubtedly, this is uniquely human, and thanks to the hypervigilance of our brain, we can deal with these ubiquitous events. Everybody dreams and thinks, but no one can see another's dreams or thoughts.

It was supposed, for millennia, as a logical extension (or wishful thinking) of human cognition that an afterlife followed everyone's journey of life on Earth. Religions promised it, societies endorsed burying rituals and laws, and all persons hoped for it with visions of a private heaven or hell, having heard and read about it and seeing it codified. For generations, no sacrifice was too great as long as hope for an afterlife endured to serve the unique human malady of a neurotic fear of what has not yet occurred. From this oldest and strongest human emotion of expectant anxiety, as opposed to palpable fear of reality, religion and godheads were born and grew exponentially toward self-destruction.

It was equally inconceivable for mankind to witness the certain loss of accumulated knowledge, unless and until each new generation was rebooted with elemental lessons of comprehension, only to add a minute increment to world knowledge before the process repeated itself. A birthing process that lacks passing a compendium of accumulated knowledge as a birthright is inefficient and painfully slow in remedying. It involves teachers, lessons, administrators, books, the internet of things (IoT), vast physical facilities and campuses, energy, and consumption of natural resources. There had to be a way to impregnate the human genome with universal knowledge for reproduction during the gestation period of nine months, but where and how?

The answer lies in externalism, a dimension that encompasses everything in the universe that already happened and wherein the past, present, and future are equally real. That now is to time as here is to space, while real versions exist in the past and future as well. In the block universe, the unconscious makes decisions, and free will is preordained, although alluding to be a humanly conscious thought and purely subjective in substance couched in presentism.

In the context of physics, each is a general view of the nature of time, and so, it follows that Paraspermya is the microbe roamer of the galaxies that possesses all thoughts, persona, and emotions of every human being who ever lived their life on Earth and has passed. Heir Nushima is forever inscribed on this oasis of humanity, forever roaming the universe at speeds greater than 6.2 miles per second relative to the speed of expanding stars that were evident long before human existence. Viewing where the cosmos are most abundant or devoid strongly suggests the origin of Paraspermya, which is completely dependent upon the souls of humanity for its energy. This permanent and growing aggregation of ancestral wisdom exists only to exert a metaphysical influence on each living human; however, they may filter it as they live on Earth.

Aliennus, the prophetic spirit of Paraspermya, arrived on Earth that day to commune with humanity by invading their psyches beyond the traditional faculty state to teach all earthlings that the past will no longer encroach on the future. Henceforth, all acquired useless and addictive pain will be purged from the human spiritual heart, also known as human will. This dream is the only means of attaining permanent world peace. Aliennus's assignment was estimated to endure for a millennium or forty sequential Earth generations. Filled with a universal database affording the identity and ancestral history of every living being, their native language, religious beliefs, archetypes, and biases, Aliennus was programmed to invoke supernatural and transformative message dreams to purge the extreme stresses and brutality of religious wars from the human condition, all during the Rapid Eye Movement (REM)sleep cycle. Not to replace free will, but to choose social structures to live within or balance present-day realities with intergenerational spiritualties. This created the need to homogenize ancient doctrines of narrow theologies with an equitable practice all mankind could enjoy. A myriad of worship methods that continued to spread chastened values around the world proves absurd in logic and pernicious in practice to prevent religious wars. The doctrine of homogenizing religion strips humanity of the long-standing quid pro quo of afterlife promises in exchange for abstract rules by which to live on Earth. The time for change had come.

Beginning with Greenwich mean time (GMT), everybody had at least one morning each day, and those insomniacs with varied life schedules or sleep disorders experienced even more. But on March 11, 2014, every adult arose from their slumber with an identical recollection of the night's dream and couldn't wait to exchange the experience with their peers. After, of course, their obligatory yawns, stretches, occasional showers, and breakfast prepared them for the encounter. At first opportunity, they burst forth with an urgent exclamation juxtaposed on the customary greeting of "good morning"; they cried, "I had the strangest dream last night!"

One can only imagine the shock and surprise when learning how ubiquitous their strange dream was.

Individual reactions ranged from subdued confusion to thoughts of spiritual awakening. The range of speculation challenged even the most articulate of people to explain this wonderment that invaded, distorted, and threatened the very core of their existence. The thought of assimilating closely held beliefs in a multigenerational deity, whose afterlife promises were unquestioningly bought into, with singular denomination is of existential trauma. Some thought it was an idea whose time had come, but most were between the horns of a dilemma about an idea never before dreamed. Yet despite vast differences in culture, language, education, and devotion, the human herd philosophy enthusiastically adopted the congenial thought of homogenizing religion. But would it survive? People change their minds all the time, but can a universal dream change people's minds permanently?

COSMIC TELEPATHY

Fr: Aliennus

To: Paraspermya

Via: Cosmic Telepathy

The initial dream assault was imputed to every living person on planet Earth on the same day as they slept.

"I know you," the dream voice said, "from the sea of humanity that surrounds you! Do you remember when you fell from a swing and broke your arm when nobody was home? How would anyone else know you cried and shivered until your collie, Sandy, placed her paw gently over your wound and licked tears from your face to comfort you? Sure, you are dreaming about that, me, and aren't past events fun to dream about? They really matter and rank high among the best memories of life. Kindnesses deserve to be stored away, honored, and often recalled. Come with me along another path of imagination called foresight that emerges when unease and discomfort are active. Everyone needs solutions when they are rankled.

"You shall participate in an enduring legacy of forever ridding Earth of the violence, bloodshed, and extreme stress of religious wars, and here's how: When you awaken, all religious traditions and practices will be expunged, sans guilt, no matter your deity of choice. This newly found capacity will enable you to better

digest the truth and wisdom of what religions intended to become before they were corrupted by faux scholars who ascribed to them layers of intermediaries and afterlife promises in exchange for absolute obedience to sacrosanct teachings that seemingly justified them. This is your chance to humanize your need of faith by ending millenniums of war caused by unfounded absolutism. Homogenizing religion is the only answer for eternal peace on Earth. So awake and enthusiastically partake in saving the world for future generations."

RELIGIOUS DEBATES THAT ENSUE

CATHOLICISM

The extraordinary assembly of interfaith bishops was hastily convened by Pope Luke II to address the pastoral challenges of evangelizing a homogenizing religion as dreamt of by shepherds and congregants alike. The excitement among them was palpable as they gathered inside the Dome of the Rock in Jerusalem. Clergy of all religions and stratifications mixed and matched with one another, scurrying about, seeking to validate another mystery; that being, the miracle of a worldwide common dream never heard of before. Prostration, prayer, and meditation were cast aside by the crazed mood and rancor in this holy place by the religious princes for whom it was built (the public was not allowed inside). The frantic activity within could be likened to a chicken coop invaded by red-headed roosters.

A committee of these titular CEOs of world religions sat upon thrones of equal stature, as they had demanded, around an ancient center mosaic with their cadre of translators dispensed with the benediction and drew lots to speak first. Luke II, the convening authority, opened the forum by declaring an unconditional endorsement of religious homogenization, but queried, "What is to become of us, intermediaries, if holy rituals are no longer needed?" Princely heads nodded in unison, not unlike the sequencing sounds of a pinball machine.

The supreme mullah spouted, "And my monthly stipend?" The chief rabbi, forefinger piercing the air, pondered in Hebrew the future of Israel as a religious state and the UJA as its monetizing benefactor. The bishop of Canterbury wondered aloud about attendance in their magnificent cathedrals and rentals for palatial pastoral homes.

The Dalai Lama, with clasped hands tight around his worry beads, exclaimed, "What of my monks and their monasteries and my private jet?"

The Russian Orthodox pope stroked his lengthy tobacco-stained white beard, postured, "*Da!*"

The Confucian monk, although not exactly an accredited religionist, was granted purchase, and he silently petitioned to exhort Hong Kong and Taiwan to merge with Mainland China.

Lastly, Luke II, hands clasped in supplication, shouted, "Can the Vatican Bank shed all those pedophile liabilities? And where is that damned Hindu?"

The meeting adjourned sine die.

Fr: Aliennus

To: Paraspermya

Via: Cosmic Telepathy

Re: Dream Reaction of Earthly Religionists

As expected, a worldwide synod was conducted in response to the dream. While compliant with the concept of homogenizing religion, it quickly became clear that the doctrine of separate and equal was uniformly invoked by most, including the Buddhist, as was the valuation, disposition, and compensation for their owned tax-free assets. Finally, there was assurance of their personal survival and stature.

Fr: Paraspermya

To: Aliennus

Via: Cosmic Telepathy

Re: Dream Reaction of Earthly Religionists

Thank you, Aliennus. It is decided; you will deliver a codicil to the dream especially crafted for all earthbound clergy as soon as possible.

Sleep was uneasy for the congregants this night. Confused by their enthusiasm for the titillating dreams, which conflicted with eons of strict linear religious training and inevitable narrow point of view, they turned and twisted, sweated and shivered until completely submerged in the REM stage. While immersed in this deep well of slumber, a dream with a religious penchant was dreamt by all synod participants—at the same time!

To: Aliennus

Fr: Paraspermya

Via: Cosmic Telepathy

Re: Delivery of a Clerical Codicil

Rejoice in obtaining forgiveness and pardon for all sins, and don't worry about your livelihood or restraints from daily duties. The time for comparative religions and their radical conflicts will fade away as your minions discard rooted seeds and learn to criticize other religions but not the people who adopted them. You, a theologian and teacher, know that all beliefs and rituals are but part of the universal religion that you now advocate for world peace. You will be revered more than parents who bring life into the world, for you can now prepare lives for a world of peace. Never give up on your dreams!

Satisfied, as only possessors of a singular theology can be, each cleric awoke from the second dream, visualizing themselves as headmasters of specialty schools within a global university where they and their peers would teach and relive the history of their religion, the only true one, including worship services for students and nostalgic laypersons who thrived on archetypes and rituals. So long, that is, as the requirement for teaching homogenizing religion was not elective. They realized that attrition of the faithful would provide the basis for adopting a future curriculum.

Endorsement was unanimous despite the ambivalence of relinquishing their adopted deity and blessed intermediary saints that stood between reality and spirituality. This resided within their core and manifested in strobe-like flashes of theirs as the only surviving religion. The ethers were filled with texting among the church participants and their minions as they sought traction for their respective theologies. Roman Catholics throughout the world swore the ubiquitous dreams foretold the second coming of Christ and admonished the clergy to mandate more serial and ritualistic masses for devout believers in hopes of surviving what was perceived as a threat to purge Christians. The bishops concluded if a homogenizing religion was to populate the world, let it be Roman Catholic! Their texts and tweets, when retrieved from permanent storage on the cloud, would crystallize their innermost thoughts and fears but end with an "aye" vote for homogenizing religion.

EARTH CABLES

To: MthrSuperior@MetroCathdeBuenosAires

Fr: Luke@VatCity

Subject: Synod

Liz, Can u believe I finally met Papa, can't bother with doctrinal changes but must deal with a new homogenizing religion? Jesus, I can't catch a break. Meeting was good. The other guys were fine but my insiders are a pain. I'll need your help with them. Talk again soon.

MnsrMarioPuzo@vatbk

Agreed with group but worried about our cash, investments & assets. Keep books (set #2) available on short notice. Don't know where this is headed. See you soon.

Emin Card Arevedecchi

AScalia@vatlegal

Check sales/leaseback files between VatBank & various Mosques, Temples, & Taj Mahal. Also cleanup all pending pedophile cases. Fan about to hit the wall.

Fondly, Card. L. Legato

Mwamba@CapetownMonestary

Pls. arrange a Southern Africa Bishop's Conference ASAP. RC missionaries will take care of rest of continent.

Card. Straightpath

Confusion among the ranks of Catholic clergy arose not from homogenizing religion but from the tribal teaching to protect mother church from controversies and intrusions into its convoluted and sequestered assets. Those conclaves were to be jealously guarded, not to be shared with the needy, destitute, or sexually abused congregants. This was the knee-jerk reaction of the church brethren to the dreams. Although acted upon every day by every cleric, these collusive acts were never evident to outliers. In fact, particular pride was encouraged among them on their individual metacognitive ability to think, act, but never communicate complex policies outside the cabal. This blind obedience to hypervigilance resulted in fear, confusion, and hypocrisy among the Roman Catholic clerics by conflicting with their individual, but uniquely human, mental tools to investigate and uncover facts—the quest of the human soul versus the man-made doctrinaire of the church.

ISLAMISM

Islamic scholars who function as legislative bodies within the religion are known for sculpturing pious rules into feasible secular dispensations. Having dreamt the dreams, they and their supreme Sunni and Shia mullahs, Abu Bakr and Abi Talib, respectively, were hard-pressed on how to reconcile their eschatological dedication between themselves and any other religion. Islam is a prophetic religion of different sects that define earthly existence as transitory to a predetermined destiny. It has little room for human freedoms, thoughts, and deeds. Islamic law is often stretched by legal scholars, including the twelve imams, for the sake of commerce, convenience, consideration of public welfare, or to strengthen juristic discretion. To prevent the Koran from being a barrier to homogenizing religion, a reconciliation of the denominations required much deliberation and discussion by the reigning supreme mullahs and their minions.

Sunni Supreme Mullah Abu Bakr meditated alone on how to temper the beliefs of 90 percent of the world's Muslim population, whose historical difference from the minority Shias rested on a base ideological belief that Prophet Muhammad anointed his father-in-law as first caliph rather than his son-in-law, Abi Talib, as believed by the Shia Islamic sect. For two millennia, breaches and consequent wars between these denominations were based on an ideological import of succession to the supreme imam of the caliphate, as evidenced by the many pseudonyms of succession taken by reigning mullahs, similar to RC popes and their saints. He distilled his wide-ranging thoughts about the great divide between the Islamic factions that proved so costly to both sects and concluded the core problem was assuring succession as a supreme mullah for each generation.

This practice was not a matter of bloodlines likened to Western monarchies, because Islamic succession was based on scholarly knowledge and commitment to a denomination. If the minions of both sects were ever to enter into a joint venture whereby they agreed to abide to an alternating supremacy that would serve for a defined time period to be determined by a combined supreme council of scholars, each sect could practice their rituals and rites with assurance of a protective umbrella, so to speak. There would be squabbles for sure, but no religious wars. This was a thought worth pursuing to protect the minority Shia sect and assure prominence of the Sunnis.

Meanwhile Ayatollah Abi Talib of the Shia tribe, a supreme leader dressed in ordinary Western-style street clothes except for a highly wound turban and darkened glasses, while continuously fondling his worry beads, intensely focused on preserving the strategic and influential positions his sect held in Iran, Pakistan, India, and Iraq. As such, Shia could influence ideological conflicts and wars with the Sunnis, although he now wondered if it was all in vain. His bias made it a difficult, if not impossible, challenge to peacefully coexist with Sunnis but was tempered by the new and haunting dream about homogenizing religion that would be experienced by everybody. Such an anomaly, however, could present a new opportunity for unity among all denominations of Islam. He decided to convene a video conference among his Koranic advisors—the twelve Shia imams, each a direct descendant of Muhammad, whose specific responsibilities defined, interpreted, and administered Islamic Shia law—and sent out an email.

To: The Twelve Imams

Fr: Ayatollah Abi Talib

Please join my video conference immediately via computer, smartphone, or tablet to brainstorm about our dreams from Allah for a homogenizing religion.

The conference went live, and the remote host soon announced, "All of Allah's holy men are present, my Ayatollah."

"*As-salamu-alaykum*, men of faith. We have much to discuss and decide today," exclaimed Ayatollah Abi Talib.

His presence was acknowledged in unison by the twelve imams, who formally replied, "*Wa-'alaykum as-salam*, Supreme Leader. We are humbled to be in your presence and advise you about Allah's dream for homogenizing religion."

The ayatollah said, "We begin then by acknowledging the dream phenomenon as Allah's command for us to work toward a homogenizing religion. This is a rare opportunity for all servants of Islam to put issues that separate us aside and band together to speak with one voice as a prominent religion on Earth."

As custom mandated all imams to assert their infallible power derived from God, they chanted, "We are the bearers of Sharia law."

Ayatollah Abi Talib began the discussion by asserting the rules of engagement: "Each scholar will please speak sequentially about how homogenizing religion affects his discipline. Afterward, we can debate freely until I decide how to proceed toward achieving what Allah's dream commands."

The first to speak was Muhammad Ismail Zabeeh, the imam of prayers. This small man, whose animated facial features were obscured by a high white turban, began by raising his eyebrows under thick framed eyeglasses, which sat upon a prominent nose. He sputtered a response between his huge handlebar mustache and lengthy gray beard, "Our five daily prayers to the prophet always begin by begging for guidance to uphold the Koran and finish by assuring Allah our destiny is in the afterlife. It is so every day for billions of devoted Muslims over thousands of years. What separates us from Sunnis and other infidels is how we uphold Allah's laws, rituals, and archetypes in this life to renew our guaranty of an afterlife with him. If the dream is Allah's way to unite us with other religions and sects, we must take every precaution to codify our daily prayers to assure our martyrdom. After all, that is what we live for."

Finding no fault with the imam of prayers, the eleven separate but equal scholars each pounded their left upper chest five times with closed fists and further emphasized their agreement by shouting "Amen!"

Rezi Aslan, the imam of fasting, who traveled far and wide to experience the techniques of fasting of other religions before settling down with five wives and twelve offspring to tend to his scholarly work, was next to speak on how this important ritual can survive homogenization.

He began by saying, "Fasting is not unique to Muslims, it is practiced by Christians, Jews, Confucianists, Hindus, and Taoists too. Islam is the only religion that binds it to sexual abstinence, female menstruation, sacrilegious speech, money handling, and violence, disciplines that should be left to the ayatollah. Fasting is for refreshing the spirit and is physically healthy and is not in conflict with homogenizing religion, a practice that satisfies Islam and many other religions."

Eleven other chest poundings occurred simultaneously followed by a cacophony of "Amen!"

Behind a stream of encomiums to Allah, the imam of pilgrimages, Mehdi Hasan, another direct descendant of a medieval imam said, "Adults who are physically and financially able to pilgrimage once in their lifetime add a dimension to their souls that is otherwise lost." The imam is a scholarly depiction of a sumo wrestler with calf muscles as thick as fire hydrants prominently emerging from a short, toga-like wrapping robe of white, which was probably a remnant of his pilgrimages. He continued, "Past centuries have witnessed mass pilgrimages or hajjes to Mecca, Medina, Karbala, and Mashhad to commemorate Shia martyrs that embolden the lives of our followers with support of their families, ancestors, and ancient imams. Other sects and religions have ancestral shrines of equal import to them. Pilgrimages are restorative practices that appear to have universal support. Of course, the holiness of a destination and shrine count most."

Chest beating and chanting continued as expected, until interrupted by another imam. "Charitable giving is both a blessing and an obligation to fulfill our social and theological requirements. Both are historically influenced by Christian notions of giving alms to the poor. Muslim scholars and those of most other religions agree about the obligatory nature of charity. These are well-documented admonitions that should cause no obstacle to homogenizing religion," said Agha Saeed, imam of *sadaqah* and *zakat* (charity), "and principal adherent of standardizing the giving of alms to the poor, often heard to say, 'Nothing is more satisfying than giving to the needy, especially when the gifts are not excessive!'"

Filling the screen was the full-face image framed by a black pillbox hat, dark beard, unkempt eyebrows, horn-rimmed glasses, and facial tics of Tehreem Hashmi, the imam of perpetual struggle (jihad), who, while appearing somewhat paranoid, shouted a formal greeting of "*salaam alaikum*" and quickly launched into his presentation. "Since our struggles in this life are but a prelude to rewards of the afterlife, where we dwell with our ancestral martyrs and vestal virgins, we disavow the corruptions of music, secular justice, homosexuality, and Sunnis to name a few. In this way, we prepare the souls of new generations in the ways of the Koran. This then is our risk of birth and reward of death. Other believers also struggle to survive in this world without any insight into the rewards of martyrdom—that, more than anything, sets us apart from them. Hard though it may be for us to respect these infidels, it will be easier for our grandchildren and great-grandchildren to eventually radicalize them into believers if we pretend to accept homogenizing religion."

"I agree, I agree," shouted the imam of tithes, Eboo Patel. "All imams depend on 20 percent *khums* from Muslim business profits as a major source of income to maintain our financial independence and occasionally parcel some of it to orphaned and handicapped believers. It has always been that way. What will become of us and our stipends under homogenizing religion? After all, the economics of an imam are complex. I am worried sick."

His admonition was greeted by the others with an earsplitting "Amen!"

The imam of goodness, Haqqul Yaqeen, a mild-mannered, low-talking scholar, spoke to the group, "*Ma'ruf* [respect] for law and order has always come from a preacher's sensibility to the rhythms and patterns of our culture and communal consensus [*ummah*]. Should the ayatollah decide to adopt homogenizing religion, and we proselytize it, it will become the source of moral and legal binding authority to all Shia Muslims."

"That is a race yet to be run," said Muhammad Mahdi, the imam of evil, who until now had held his thoughts private. "How the haram [sin] of homogenizing religion will resonate with the faithful is yet to be seen," he said, and continued, "The prophet Muhammad mandated that evil, once recognized, must be challenged by direct action or by at least speaking out against it and fighting against it with every fiber of your being. Today, only the ayatollah, holy is he, can declare jihad against an evil and speak out against it. We, as mullahs, can only reject what is reprehensible within our hearts. Our leaders must be on guard with a homogenizing religion."

In the silence across cyberspace, one could hear a pin drop. It was broken by the ayatollah, who said, "The hazan calls us to prayer! After we pay homage to Allah and eat lunch, we will reconvene to hear admonitions from our remaining four brethren, the imam of love, the imam of disassociation, the imam of martyrdom, and the imam of holy days. Then we will have a roundtable discussion, and I will decide on how Islam will assimilate with homogenizing religion."

The minion rose from their devices, picked up their prayer rugs, and retired.

Upon resuming the discourse, the imam of love (for Allah) said, "It is written that Allah gives only good news to his servants, and our dream of homogenizing religion is just such a miracle. We should not seek rewards for adopting his will, as we, the direct descendants of martyred imams, earned the right to spread goodness and love of the Koran and supplicate ourselves to the holy dream in gratitude."

The imam of disassociation (with Sunnis) followed with a plea, "We, the imamate body, inheritors of risala [wisdom], apostolate protectors of Islam, stipulate what the next generation of imams [our relatives] must do to overcome the obstacles to our family right from all enemies of the Shia caliphate, from whom we disassociate. The Doctrine of Tabarra dictates isolation from such minions. From ancient history to today, when we identify and disassociate faux idols and their women as the worst creations, we must continue to admonish them and their progeny as cursed Sunnis! Homogenizing religion with these pagans requires more than a dream. We Shia must have a declaration of immunity from Sunni teachings and customs, from Allah through his messengers, Muhammad and our esteemed ayatollah. Only then can we integrate."

The gathering paused to change from chest-beating into self-flogging rituals while chanting repeatedly, "Only then can we integrate!"

Calm resumed upon the appearance of Muhammad Ayub on the connected monitors. The imam of martyrdom, a low talker with a silken voice of a prophet, said in an ethereal voice, "Dreaming and martyrdom have a love affair, for it is in the state of unconsciousness that we contact past martyrs to understand the import of their sacrifices and extract what they portend for our future. The Koran declares the ultimate purpose behind our dreams is the singular insight into the heartfelt truth of Islam not available to us while awake. This dream of homogenizing religion motivates our moral and spiritual development and comes to each of us from our ancient martyrs, blessed be them, the predictors of our future. We must follow it!"

Afterward, a collective sigh and head-nodding emanated from the participants (including the ayatollah), but the silence was broken by the words of the imam of holy days. "One-half of our sixteen annual holy days are inviolate, those being, Eid al-Fitr, Eid al-Adha,

Islamic New Year, birthdays of Muhammad and Ayatollah Abi Talib, Ramadan, and the hajj. These must remain sacred. Those faithful servants of Allah who desire to celebrate other holidays can do so in the privacy of their homes or at local mosques. By preserving them, we can endure a homogenizing religion."

Having heard from the supporting imams and skeptics of how to convert a dream anomaly into a reality, the supreme ayatollah planned a roundtable discussion the next day to craft the disparate group into homogeneous adherents to homogenizing religion to the best of his ability, with help from Aliennus.

A DREAM CODA FOR ISLAMISTS

As descendants of the prophets Muhammad, Adam, Abraham, Moses, and Jesus—all of whom are considered as messengers of divine intervention by Islam, and despite your fierce belief in monotheism—the time has come for you and all people of Earth to pay homage to ancestors who struggled to define a higher power as the only answer to the unanswerable. Yet scholars and scientists of past centuries have chipped away at many mysteries so successive generations accepted them as unquestioned realities. And although many answers remain to be revealed, the pattern is clearly established. It is only a matter of time when perception overrules superstition. And so it is with religious apprehensions. They, too, must be tethered to the universe, because religious wars on Earth produce inordinate stress on other galactic bodies by distorting the equanimity of dark matter that balances the stress of all matter, living or innate, in the universe.

This existential condition must end by homogenizing religion. As thinking creatures, you realize the seriousness of this condition regardless of your beliefs that have heretofore served as comfort for the unanswerable. This solution will ensure succession of your species and provide you with a cognitive solution to life's mystery between an unknown beginning and an unimaginable end. And one more thing before you awake: trivializing the mutual dependence of male and female genders and ascribing it to religion is absurd in human logic and pernicious in practice. Women's subservience to men festers violence. Do something about it when you awaken!

At 7:00 a.m. the next day, thirteen pairs of eyes snapped open, hearts beating uniformly rapid, hands tearing at beards, and legs thrashing as though in spasm. Imams shouted favored curses, spewed invectives incoherently until exhausted, afterward retreating to their bathrooms to brush their facial hair, tie their turbans, and otherwise prepare for the ayatollah's webinar, where they swore to vent their angst and wonderment, not knowing of the dream's universality.

At the prescribed time, the conference commenced with everyone eager to participate.

The ayatollah began, "Last night, Allah's messenger came to me in my sleep once again to confide in me—"

He was roundly interrupted by almost all the participants, who reacted urgently and in sync, "Me too!"

Somewhat flustered, the ayatollah blurted, "Once again we had the same dream at the same time? Islamists are truly the chosen people to receive from Allah the only way to assure our martyrdom by homogenizing religion to preserve Earth for all mortals and disown violence. These are the pathways to the immortality we seek." Amid several interruptions, the ayatollah continued, "I have heard your opinions and want to address the concerns you raised, including preserving five daily prayers, retaining annual holidays and pilgrimages, fear of lost tithes, and most of all, assurance that we Shia remain protected against the dreaded Sunnis. I want to help assuage you of all these concerns right now."

Almost as a chorus, the imams replied, "Supreme Leader, we, too, had the dream and agree that homogenizing religion is the right way for Islam. There is no need to discuss it, as we will find solutions for our concerns. What we are upset about is granting equal rights for women. For that, we will go to war!"

The ayatollah patted his brow and heaved a sigh of relief.

JUDAIC KABBALISTS

An uncompromised humanity was nonnegotiable for all Jews given their history as the oppressed, expelled objects of genocide. For these reasons, they were least impressed by the ubiquitous dream of homogenizing religion. In fact, they were frightened to abandon their Jewish state of Israel, the protection of Western powers, and cadre of generational donors. The past century was the most peaceful time in history for the Jews. Despite incidental threats, there were no existential actions to plague them. If anything, they were unrelenting victims of religious wars, not perpetrators. Quick to adapt and survive changing environments, the chief rabbi of this new century and his minions sought a path that least risked repudiation of their sacred and treasured designation as the chosen people. Homogenizing religion posed such a dilemma to kabbalists for over four generations, and so they suffered in silence.

Kabbalah is an esoteric discipline that attempts to define the mysterious nature of the universe and that of humans. Its origin predates organized religions and is ripe with occultist adaptations of generations of self-ordained sages, prophets, and fabulists. One imagines a parallel to the populist tales of Aesop described in a famous poem:

THE FABULIST

About 600 BC, mythology got a boost
when a story-teller's fame required a repertoire
of tantalizing tales to keep an audience seduced

or his career was through.
This was the age of prolific canards that
inspired imagination, taught people morality,
and yet still entertained.

laughter and humor still reigned.
One such fabulist, Aesop by name,

taught morality with stories of animals
with human personalities.

So prolific were his allegories
that no two tales posed a similarity.

Aesop's fables were performed only in Greece
and lasted 250 years, orally passed on with ease.

At banquets, Philocleon, the Roman elder
spun many a tale

Socrates the philosopher,
heard about them while in jail:

The Fox & The Lion left them crying
A Wolf in Sheep's Clothing

gave them cause for sighing.
The Tortoise and the Hare
was how to race to the finish.

From generation to generation,
over a great span of time,

Aesop's fables survived without one written line,
To become the Greek national pastime.

By 370 BC, 250 years later, hundreds of these
fables were still acted out and heard.

Then a nobleman, Demetrius of Phalerum,
transcribed into prose that when read aloud seemed quite absurd.
Orators of the day performed over 600 recitations
to captive audiences without repetition due to Aesop's human-like herd.

Fast-forward to 25 AD (650 years later), a Roman fabulist,
Phaedrus-a-kup, translated them into Latin iambic tetrameter poems,
but lost their pathos, exuberance, rhythmic beats and humorous tones.
Yet latinizing opened new forums, causing quite a fervor.

Soon other orators translated Phaedrus' core,
but none would ever match Aesop by their incursion,
His ethics and morality undid the butchery and banality
of Jewish law and Christian liturgy.

Aesop's fables are used to teach Biblical lore,
By obscuring banal disciplines and metaphors,
which obscure moral maxims and social mores,
that endure today and forevermore.

The theosophical traditions of the theoretical Kabbalah sought to understand and describe the realm of divinity by using abstractions that, at best, were understood intuitively to harbor the secrets of creating the universe and forces of nature. Such mythic and mystical speculations rose to the level of religion when sustained by legendary tales as Moses encountering a burning bush or receiving the Ten Commandments at Mount Sinai around the thirteenth century BCE. For the most part, esoterism formed the basis for Judeo-Christian mystical beliefs over millennia and for numerous generations. Homogenizing religion is antithetical to witnessing their ultimate purpose for living; that being, the coming of the Messiah and his holy promise to eliminate war, destruction, and man's inhumanity to man. Who needed a dream while waiting for a messiah? And so, a few courageous adherents of the ancient Kabbalah set out to attempt to reconcile their hidden beliefs and mystical tenets that ended with the same promise of peace in the dream.

Rabbi Avraham Azula, a proponent of demystifying Kabbalic teachings, came from a lineage of male rabbis and Talmudic and Kabbalah scholars. He was, however, among the first to witness the ordination of female rabbinical and cantorial celebrants during the twenty-first century until the year 2014, when the chaos after the first universal dream essentially replaced formalized prayer sessions of most of the 4,200 earthly religions. Far from demanding the supernal purity of the Kabbalah as others did, he decided long ago its hidden teachings were complimentary to the mystery of a godhead. To him, the Kabbalah secrets were part of a central metaphor of a psychological need for mankind's collective soul to unite or divide the harmony of creation. The dream offered no less a choice between heaven and hell. Rabbi Azula ended his discourse by stating, "It is not the god of the Kabbalah that changes; it is our perception of him that must change."

Ramban Nahmanides was an esteemed Talmudic scholar descended from the grand Sephardic rabbi Moses ben Nahman Gironde, who lived in the first millennium and who was known for his commentaries that connected the teachings of the Kabbalah directly to the Old Testament. Ramban cited the insightfulness of his more recent predecessors to that task as well as comparing the teachings of the Kabbalah to the existential threat of the dream, and so began his monologue: "According to the Torah, humanity is the foundation of the universe, separated from all other creatures by morality, ethical justice, and mercy. But these pillars of our existence become immoral in the extreme. The Talmud stresses that in the absence of righteousness, God is hidden and all creation ceases. The Kabbalah teaches us metaphorically that it is the tree of life and knowledge that empowers us to receive supernal divinity by 'doing to others, as we would have them do to us.' This religious attribute extends across the universe and is in harmony with the consequences of the dream."

No sooner had Ramban ended his soliloquy than Rabbi Bahya ben Asher began speaking with a tonal quality almost indistinguishable from that of Rabbi Ramban, "Ramban, you come from a scholarly lineage that has, for millennia, tried to fit the Kabbalah into the ancient Torah, and now you are trying to fit it into the dream. I, on the other hand, continue to believe the Torah evolved into the Kabbalah, and that has yet to find comity with the dream." Rabbi Asher continued, "The difference between us is in defining evil!"

Mouth agape, Ramban eeked, "Evil? Rabbi Asher, there is no place for evil in the Torah, Kabbalah, or the dream. Changes, rules, rituals, yes—all as guides for goodness."

"Aha, that is where we differ, Ramban," said Rabbi Asher. "I can prove the Torah is bound to Kabbalah by the nature and origin of evil as much as it is with holiness, both qualities of God. Without evil, truth and God cease to exist. Often conceived as demonic, evil is a mythical parallel to holiness that protects goodness by curbing overzealous imports about its purity. My problem is, I can't find a place for evil in the dream. Perhaps it will appear one day?"

A preeminent Kabbalic sage, Rabbi Moshe Idel spoke in a mellifluous voice that belied his advanced age but confirmed his esteemed stature in Judaism. He began, "All beliefs, whether religious or not, contain misconceptions and other flaws. The Kabbalah is ripe with them, as is the Talmud. A tried-and-true remedy used by Kabbalists to atone for these imperfections is the promise of an afterlife experience, though not written in the Bible or rabbinic literature and generally rejected by most Jewish scholars. The Kabbalah, however, implies a mystique of reincarnation with a number of philosophical stipulations of guilt that must be overcome during a lifetime. They have to do with the human soul." He paused. "Perhaps when and if the dreamt concept of homogenizing religion is codified, the promise of an afterlife will also rely on intentions rather than practices? Think how unifying it would be if the Kabbalah and homogenizing religion coalesced with the hope of an afterlife."

Rabbi Idel went on, "Evidence beyond a reasonable doubt is more important here than any form a promise of an afterlife takes. For example, the Kabbalah describes in copious detail how people rise to the level of deserving. We are all scholars of religious law, and I will condense this evolutionary scale to compare what we should expect from homogenizing religion. Reincarnation is described in the Kabbalah as the transmigration of the soul after death from a primordial act of imparting the soul of life to a newborn [nefesh] and developing it in staged levels over a lifetime. At thirteen years of age, upon Bar Mitzvah, the second level of understanding, kedushah, is reached in preparation of successive levels, and if acquired, moral virtue [ruach], intellect [neshama], awareness of a deity [*chayyah*], acceptance of god [*yehidah*], and the life force needed as a reminder, as in *yeseira*, the weekly Sabbath. These are the steps required for reincarnation, according to the Kabbalah. The form of the promised afterlife is not described, but one would think it an ephemeral or spiritual compression for all mankind. At least, I do! Now can we adjourn until tomorrow as we reflect and sleep on how to reconcile our religious passions with homogenizing religion?"

DREAM CODA FOR KABBALISTS

Your struggle for recognition over the ages when faced with the totality of a religion was only within the margin of error of the world's census and was bound to eventually transform survival defenses into violent aggression. Long-term suffering, as you and your ancestors endured, obscured this transformation for generations. Once uncovered, however, the Jewish people of Earth began to search for answers and redemption by scouring their sacred books that codified the serial interpretation of basic tenets upon which religion is built. Thus, the Kabbalah clarified the confusion and conflicts among Torah, Talmud, and Kabbalistic knowledge and understandings. The devotion of these scholars was to follow right the comparisons of gaping voids and hasty remedies redacted by the ancients, hoping to redeem the promise of the Ten Commandments, which your people revere or try to.

These efforts never went unnoticed. Rather they influenced parallel generations of other religions. Some even adopted them without attribution of course. Nevertheless, the effect of this moral compass on civilization reduced or delayed religious violence over the millennia that would otherwise have been much worse much sooner. The value of dispersion and influence of Jews among the world population is greatly underrated as a moral suasion. Recently, however, the Jewish people coalesced into a single nation-state. The unseen consequence of which was to dissolve the influence of teaching and remind others of the sacrifices endured and lessons taught by you for world peace and replace it with an explosion of violence to defend yourselves against unspeakable aggression by other Semitic religions that threatened your existence. The very same religions that shared many of your principles resented their adaptation and, in the process, removed all estoppels against violence to gain prominence for their uninitiated beliefs. The stress emanating from millennia of religious wars affects the universe by distorting the balance of dark matter among galaxies and could birth more of or larger black holes. Such a universal imbalance can't be sustained, and the likelihood of lasting world peace is doubtful. Homogenizing religion is the only remedy remaining to mankind for world peace and avoids a cataclysmic omnicide.

Kabbalist scholars and all Judaism dreamt the same dream again at the same time and awoke to unconditionally adopt homogenizing religion for their salvation. Acceptance was as much an act of conscience as resistance, where faith is more a conviction of humanity and, therefore, a good deal more fastidious on Earth than in any imaginative heaven. It was no surprise that given the capacity for self-appraisal in the Hebrew Bible, religious beliefs that stand against custom or consensus can, nevertheless, emanate as matters of conscience or as a continuum of righteousness so central to the Old Testament.

CHRISTIANITY

Christian denominations rooted in Judeo-Christian theology are far from unified, except they all agree on Jesus as a common point of reference. Competition for believers among Baptists, Methodists, Fundamentalists, and Scientologists cause splintering despite similar views in trinity theism, resurrection, and eternal salvation and damnation. The bishop of Canterbury, titular head of White Anglo-Saxon Protestants (WASPs), nonetheless habitually counseled all church bodies in the Christian denominational pluribus via video calls. Their self-interests in preserving eleemosynary assets, pastoral privileges, tax-free cash flows, and lay employment that protected them from working were common topics. While all denominations tacitly adopted harmonizing religion after the dream, much work was needed to completely convert them. To work on this, they convened at Westminster Abbey to assuage one another and conspire to mitigate the personal sacrifices they would endure by losing their exclusive franchises.

In one sect or another, Christianity flourished somewhere in the world for three millennia, having found its roots by translating Hebrew texts into Latin. One of the most influential compilations of these manuscripts produced a transliteration of the mystery of a living Hebraic trinity of the elemental, celestial, and intellectual into a Christian transmigration of post-death souls meeting the Father, Son, and Holy Ghost. These euphemistic Christian *truths* were first recognized as improvements to the Judaism depicted in the Hebrew Kabbalah soon to be rewritten, adopted, and Latinized by Christians as a Kabbalah Denudata. That was early in the second millennium.

Eventually, this appendage from Judaism faded as it became commonplace but wound up as a perceived threat to Christianity, a metamorphosis that took place over the second millennium. Appreciation of the Judeo-Christian connection resumed in the year AD 2014 when the concept of homogenizing religion was popularized, because Christianity became a general movement with no de facto, universal governing authority. Its many factions, while trying to share a common history, relied on denominational hierarchies within two distinct linguistic divisions: Latin in the west and Aramaic in the east. To accomplish this, an ecumenical was held at the abbey not to gain a better understanding among the many denominations of Christianity nor launch a syncretism among the church families, which included Lutherans, Coptic Christians, Evangelicals, Pentecostals, Protestants, Eastern Orthodox, Mormons, and Jehovah's Witnesses. The purpose of this synod was to respond to the first common dream and adopt a doctrine of indifference, describing protocols that would provide clear, visible, and organic acceptance of homogenizing religion. Thus proposed, the council adjourned until the next day. The participants left for the evening and retired to a night of dreams.

DREAM CODA FOR CHRISTIANS

Homogenizing religion restores equilibrium on Earth by refining human values, avoiding religious violence, assuring world peace, and restoring equilibrium to the universe. Let's face it, Christianity always reserved a place for violence and justified it by manipulating central tenets of love and peace to avenge the crucifixion and proselytize with the sign of the cross, witch hunts, murdered heretics, inquisitions, crusades, pagan slaves, tithing, lack of empathy for the poor, and more. The cumulative stress and anxiety caused by each act of violence radiates throughout the earth and dark matter, and the resulting chaotic displacement stresses by birthing more or larger black holes. All religious franchises that empower these threats to humanity were dissolved. Faith practices come from lingering consciousness, but rich ideas are the work of sound sleepers . . . and dreamers!

Resumption of the ecumenical conference the day after the dreams included unanimous rejection of sectarian earthly concerns and adoption of homogenizing religion.

BUDDHISM

Buddhism is a nontheistic religion concerned with living. Heaven, or nirvana, is here on Earth with no deity to promise afterlife rewards. The route to reincarnation of the Buddha, however, is varied and lengthy, depending on the path followed by different sects and subsects. The dream of consolidation by homogenizing religion was particularly attractive to Binatzu, the living Dalai Lama, so long as he was convinced the earthly wisdom, ethics, and reality that the Buddhist ideas preached to devotees for two millennia would survive.

Binatzu posited, "When I awake each morning and wipe the sleep from my eyes and my racing heart slows, I know the answer is in the dream. After all, Buddha reached the same conclusion long ago and went on to teach how everybody can reach nirvana, or individual happiness, and achieve world peace to fight the war of the terror of the gods. Now, I realize how painstaking the stress of religious wars are, some of which were caused by self-righteous fundamentalism in Southern Asia. When asked to reject religious quietism for community activism, monks reacted with anti-progressive violence. We lost our way, and it was felt throughout the universe! My ancestors, the forty-one other Dalai Lamas, knew that moral suasion alone would never gain purchase as a mass philosophy for peace on Earth, and thus the emphasis on individuality. This universal dream proves we needed a good way to convince anyone and everyone that religious wars must end, and now, I think we have it!

"Although convinced after the dream, I felt a need for some validation from my religious peers and decided to place a conference call to Aung San Suu Kyi in Myanmar and B. R. Ambedkar in India. Their clocks are only two and a half hours earlier than here in Tibet.

It was Aung San Suu Kyi's father, Aung Suu, who was my old friend, but he was killed shortly after Myanmar gained independence from Britain with his help. His daughter inherited his talent and intellect, both of which was nurtured by her mother who was a political activist. Today she is my closest confidant on Buddhist matters.

"B. R., on the other hand, comes from a long line of Indian political leaders and, while ten years younger than Aung San Suu Kyi, is a devout Buddhist and good friend to both of us."

As I placed the call, I thought, *I trust them both.*

"Hello, Suu Kyi and B. R., this is Binatzu, I am in Tibet today and need to talk with you about the dream we had in our native languages and at the same time. I am still reeling from the experience and unsettled about how the role of Buddhism will change."

"Binatzu, thank you for your call. After having dreamt the dream, I awoke confused yet strangely sanguine," said Suu Kyi. "My biggest concern is that we and our followers will be alienated from all others under homogenizing religion."

"Right on, Suu Kyi," said B. R. "Precisely because of our extreme self-reliance to improve ourselves and live happily, how can we fit into a potpourri of religions arising from imaginings, arcane laws, behavioral and dietary rules, and books from which to live by?"

Binatzu answered, "Of course, you're both right to be skeptical as I am. But after thinking it over and listening to you, I am reminded of one of our adages, 'Thousands of candles can be lit from one without shortening its life.' Do you recall it?"

In unison, they replied, "Yes!"

B. R. added, "That is true, but while our religion is best suited to homogenizing religion, we hope for a more convincing explanation as to its real purpose."

"Let's sleep on it and talk again tomorrow," said Binatzu, feeling that the conversation was optimistic and inspiring.

Meanwhile, a community of Buddhist monks assembled to discuss the deeper meaning of the universal dream, because Buddha did not set out to create rules for his monks to live by and admonished them in the Bhikku Patimokkha toward self-discipline arising from specific incidents of common behavior. One example of which is masturbation, common among all religious communities that practice celibacy. Following lengthy communal discussion, it was agreed to be banned for it was performed by "the same hand used for eating gifts from the faithful." Their angst was due to no mention of any depraved conduct.

DREAM CODA FOR BUDDHISTS

Why suffer from fear of alienation when your beliefs are left to each individual, and salvation is solely dependent upon them? You are right that nothing in the universe deserves your love more than you, so continue to live in the moment—become whatever you want, encourage others, and coax your conscience to be clear every day so the joy of homogenizing religion will be in your shadow for life.

Upon wakening, the Dalai Lama, his disciples, and all of Buddhism agreed to be unconditional adherents of homogenizing religion after first ordaining women's right to inhabit any Buddhist monastery in Saudi Arabia, Canada, Japan, Bangladesh, India, Ethiopia, Senegal, and Mongolia. These reforms were now mandated in the very cultural religious context that gave rise to this pervasive gender discrimination in the first place. Namaste!

COPTIC CHRISTIANS

Eastern Orthodoxy is an autocephalous religious group separated by two hundred different but equal canonical segments throughout the world. These apocryphal bishops counseled patriarch Sebastian Krill on their concerns about homogenizing religion before he embarked on his journey to the synod. Upon his return, he briefed his comrades on the perception of the symposium toward genuine unity and their plans to eradicate the schisms that exist within the church-at-large by homogenizing religion in a way they could participate. As Bishop Pyotr of Novgorod put it, "Only the heritage of Eastern Orthodoxy retains the culture of each eparchy while practicing a worldwide religion."

Bishop Arcady of Constantinople mused, "After all we've been through from the beginning of 866 CE through the first millennium filled with paganism, and through the second millennium manifested by the Mongol invasion and Tartar oppression, to modern times under Communism and Stalin, and now still fighting to survive, we are looked on as the de facto state religion under Putin. This leader subsumes our rich liturgy and theology to his political needs, corrupting our eyes and hearts, which are no longer drawn to heaven through the onion domes of our grand cathedrals."

"This dream of homogenizing religion can be the saving grace to prevent suffering of future generations, all for the sake of reincarnation that we pray for," bellowed Bishop Mstislav of Kiev.

Patriarch Krill had the last word. "Let us retire to consider our fate when earthly time overtakes divinity, as it surely must. We will reconvene tomorrow."

DREAM CODA FOR COPTIC CHRISTIANS

Your religion, since its founding, is bound together by sharing a divine essence, ousia, among the faithful. One that is without a beginning or end and therefore strictly spiritual. Your scripture even defines ousia as the prominent coalescing force of a Holy Trinity of three individual persons, the hypostases, and is therefore infinitely divisible. This same doctrine holds that the free will of mankind is interlaced with sin to which forgiveness is innate. These very tenets are the everlasting value you add to the universe for the use of free-willed future generations. Homogenizing religion preserves these liturgies, except for the dispensations, while nice, don't rewrite history. Thus, the immortality of all your orthodox practitioners is assured.

Patriarch Krill presided when the synod reconvened and began his homily to the bishops. "Brothers, I had a dream last night about ousia and hypostases and how we can preserve them by homogenizing religion."

The bishops rose as one, bound by their ousia, to announce, "We had the same dream!"

Krill fell to his knees, in awe of experiencing another dream targeting his flock. He was sure it included every Roman Orthodox member in the world, and then he pronounced to the bishops, "We now experienced two dream messages together, which, by itself, is miraculous. Here on Earth, under Putin, we sacrificed the free will of our constituents to become a state religion and survive. By themselves, the miracles of the dreams are powerful adherents for homogenizing religion. Yet when we consider the sacrifices we make to exist, we know there must be a better way. And so, I endorse homogenizing religion." To which the congregation agreed.

CONFUCIANISM

The Confucian monk Li Kong was a direct descendant of Confucius now in his eighty-third iteration. He had volunteered to have his DNA tested in 2009 by Professor Byron Sykes of Oxford University but was vetoed by the presiding Confucian authorities, who listed his birth in the records declaring Kong's place in the genealogy. His temple relied on charity and was always short of funds, so he traveled alone from Taiwan to attend the synod and had nobody to converse with for perspective or counsel. As a separate but equal attendee, he was left alone to ponder the philosophical advantages of homogenizing religion and the effect on the legacy of his ancestors. Only a profound event such as a universal dream could liberate him by reversing the priorities of a contemplative, monastic way of thinking more and acting less. Li Kong filled the vacuity in his mind from what he perceived as heaven with a resolution to change. His mind changed a long-standing premise that envisioned his body as inside his mind. He was shaken by the dream when he realized life could suddenly become inexplicably extinguishable by religious wars, without notice or debate from, theocratic governments. Humanity could be everlasting, however, by homogenizing religion. Of this, he was convinced.

HINDI

The Hindus showed up late. And it's no wonder, because electing a representative to the synod was discussed among a cluster of believers whose pathways were comparable to those found in an ant hill. Eventually, they produced the eminent Hindi scholar Bharata Chandogya.

Traversing the distance between New Delhi and Jerusalem was no easy task for Bharata. Indian trains ran intermittently, roads were awash, planes delayed by missing parts, and ships rerouted into unchartered waters to unload contraband cargo. In a religion pervaded by local customs, godheads, enriched tales, and stratified classes, to experience a common dream and obtuse concept of homogenizing anything instantly dissolves class-consciousness, promotes regional harmony, and thereby gains enthusiastic adherents.

Bharata was raised in India, a multicultural environment heavily influenced by the occupation and partitioning of India into Pakistan and Kashmir by their common occupier, Great Britain. He was frequently exposed to class and religious conflicts and managed to acquire a passive resistance to overt opposition and rebellion of any sort between governing powers and civil society, and thus maintained calmness during serial changes. He was convinced that behind it all lurked cronyism and corruption too extensive for real reform short of a religious revolution. His dream of homogenizing religions and the peace it promised were convincingly apparent, and he thought he could defend this change with his life. His scholarly introspection prepared him well to fathom this rare and unique solution for the peace that he dreamed. He meditated that nature and biology provided mankind with a brain, but the revelations of dreams turned it into a mind.

This dream of homogenizing religions was likened to a grain of sand on Earth that outdistanced the galaxies to answer an age-old question of how to achieve lasting peace. His divinity professors acknowledged the strange but sincere behavior and attributes of all 4,200 religions that failed to end religious conflicts. This caused him to recognize that evolution must come from hypervigilant imaginings of the mind, giving birth to a universally large, metacognitive dream, or by a dream giving birth to a mindset for survival of humanity. Until that was figured out, Chandogya continued to collude with his imaginary deities.

He concluded that no religion, even his, would ever promote the welfare of the world without bias and set his mind on the parallel path of liberality, asceticism, and truth as prevails in the law.

A BIBLIOPHILIC DIDACTUS
FOR SCHOLARS

THE DEBATE

The following is a transcript of the international religion debate:

Announcer 1: Al Jazeera, in cooperation with major TV news networks, BBC, CNN 1, CNN 2, CNN 3, and NPR, proudly presents a debate among renowned biblical scholars of Christianity, Judaism, and Islam about the pros and cons of homogenizing religion. Each participant will take part in rebuking and endorsing this new world order. Time constraints precluded inviting other theologians to participate.

Announcer 2: NoMonkeyBusiness Surveys will poll an attitudinal sample of our mixed international audience before and after the debate. The biggest change of attitude will determine the degree of enlightenment. We welcome the debaters, Professor Wail Halas, PhD., a Magill University scholar of Islamic law and Islamic intellectual history; Professor Rosemary R. Radford, a Pacific College of Christian Theology; and Lilith Night, a descendant of the Hebraic, mythical wife of Adam and the first feminist on Earth.

Announcer 1: The debaters were chosen for their experience, knowledge, and courage in divulging the invisible history of humanity. Each, in their own time, publicly pleaded against the fundamental canons and symbols of their religious hierarchy. The debate will focus on three propositions: One, do you believe religion is the cause of war? Two, do you believe your religion causes war? And three, do you believe homogenizing religion will bring world peace?

Announcer 2: Each debater will open by summarizing their conclusion about each proposition and, in rebuttal, will characterize the doubts of their conclusion. Let us begin with Professor Halas.

Professor Halas: I conclude that religious differences cause wars, but that is not the case with Islam. If the world would adopt the doctrines of the Koran, peace on Earth would soon follow. By that, I mean Islam is more than a religion; it is a way of life. For example, while it is true that the basis of all Islamic society is the Koran, and all social intercourse conforms to it, there is no need for contracts of any sort or lawyers, as disputes are settled by Islamic scholars on the narrow scope of conformity or nonconformity to the Koran. Circumventive processes for the sake of economic necessity, however, are common among Islamic jurist scholars. Unjustified enrichment and hazardous risks of lending constitute ethical rejections. Quantification and holistic practice is part of all arrangements made among individuals and industrial entities. Islam provides remedies for social ailments. Despite my recent dreams, I don't believe that homogenizing religion would end wars any better than Islamization. So I vote yes on proposition one, no on proposition two, and no on proposition three.

Professor Radford: My opinion is that religion doesn't cause wars. Most adherents practice their faith to avoid conflicts. A smattering of extremists manage to corrupt a faith for their own selfish purposes by causing trouble. It boggles my mind how Christianity can cause wars when it implores the faithful to "turn the other cheek." My dreams convince me that homogenizing religion is right for the world. However, I am not prepared to completely abandon my Christian ethos. It's not a matter of proselytizing, but my faith excuses trespasses while alive and promises resurrection after death. With a family of saints, angels, priests, and nuns, Christianity offers charity to the poor, kindness to the sick, and honors the wealthy and healthy who contribute. Of course, we build edifices that are bazaar to the Son of God, who possessed nothing material. Somehow, we are subliminally bribing the Lord to assure he keeps his promises to us because otherwise, we have no recourse if disappointed. I vote no on proposition one, no on proposition two, and yes on proposition three.

Madame Night: My ancestors were at the beginning, and I can attest that more people kill and are killed in the name of a superior religion since the mythical beginning of religion. Why? There is nothing more painful to people than inequality, and we gave up the garden of Eden for it. The small band of our host Hebrews survived attempts at extermination by their cunning, but that was later viewed as an existential threat to a newer faith that practiced anti-Semitism. Homogenizing religion is an answer to ending wars and restoring the garden of Eden, or Israel, for those like me and all others. Therefore, I vote yes on proposition one, no on proposition two, and yes on proposition three. The obstacle in making this commitment that we Jews unanimously agree to is a fear most difficult for us to overcome. Are we ready to realize the powerful dreams of homogenizing religion despite this fear of retribution for abandoning the admonitions, commandments, and multitude of sacrifices made over two millenniums to preserve our personal God? The answer is a resounding yes, if for no other reason than to prevent my descendants from experiencing a history of defensive brutality to assure their perpetuity.

NoMonkeyBusiness Poll Results				
	Before Debate		After Debate	
Proposition 1: Do you believe religion is the cause of war?	Yes No	66% 33%	Yes No	66% 33%
Proposition 2: Do you believe your religion causes war?	Yes No	0% 100%	Yes No	0% 100%
Proposition 3: Do you believe homogenizing religion will bring world peace?	Yes No	66% 33%	Yes No	66% 33%

Fr: Aliennus

To: Paraspermya

Via: Cosmic Telepathy

Re: Dream Reaction of Religious Scholars

The galactic dream had a limited but favorable influence on biblical scholars, each of who are immersed in justifying their beliefs as more righteous than any B other dogma. The poll suggests an understanding of how religions in general caused violence and wars but overwhelmingly exculpates their own to blame all others. This narrow conclusion is somewhat mitigated by the insight conveyed in the dream that the solution to religious wars is homogenizing religion. More work is needed here to assuage this notion.

Fr: Paraspermya To: Aliennus

Via: Cosmic Telepathy

RE: Dream Reaction of Religious Scholars

Based on our collective wisdom, your observation is indeed a correct one. The decision is to proceed with a second dream to all biblical scholars and closely monitor their progress. Execute a dream coda specifically for biblical scholars.

DREAM CODA FOR BIBLICAL SCHOLARS

Your scholarly pursuit to gain universal wisdom is the only sense that is not inborn. The seed for universal wisdom, however, was planted long ago and can grow into world harmony by homogenizing religion. Since the beginning, a religion of one seemed like madness to another, so many tried for peace and failed. There are many religions that make the faithful hate but not one that makes them love. The world is left with an abundance of pseudo beliefs that pass as sacred knowledge, yet religion leads to less faith in heaven than hell. Each of the 4,200 religions on Earth behaves strangely—martyrs are praised for their courageous death, and wars are viscerally felt by the most vulnerable. Religious platitudes make the paths to war less bitter and raises human pain to the only authentic currency of man's deadly pursuits to justify seeking out medical cures and to prove political responsibility for a point of view. The reality of continuous sorrow, however, remains the legacy of myriad religious beliefs.

The subsequent poll was even more illuminating:

NoMonkeyBusiness Poll Results	
	After Dream
Proposition 1: Do you believe religion is the cause of war?	Yes 90% No 10%
Proposition 2: Do you believe your religion causes war?	Yes 80% No 20%
Proposition 3: Do you believe homogenizing religion will bring world peace?	Yes 95% No 5%

A PHILOSOPHIA MORALIS

FORUM FOR PHILOSOPHERS

With emphasis on how world morality can deal with this new phenomenon, a cluster of postmodern philosophers gathered in Montevideo, Uruguay. Present at the symposium were the following professors: Dr. Juergen Habermas of Germany, Dr. Tesfaye Ketsela of Ethiopia, Dr. T. U. Weiming of China, Dr. U. G. Krishnamurti of India; and Dr. Enrique Dussel of Argentina and Mexico.

Each would bring their philosophical expertise to bear on the dilemma of integrating all philosophies, including trans-modernism, the need for consensus, the humanistic spirit, linguistic intersubjectivity, and the world mind. They would seek common ground and hope to opine unanimously to the world an approach to this unique experience.

Professor Weiming began the discourse, saying, "History is filled with rash, unexpected events, and so we have another unexplained phenomenon, or something more, in the news for a week. And who takes seriously any thought of humanity voluntarily giving up their religious intentions?" He then expounded on the timeliness of thinking beyond an enlightened mentality and continued, "Assuming arguendo, one could embark upon the most powerful ideology in world. I'm suggesting it could be the only option for a future of the human community."

Professor Habermas tacitly agreed with him and proposed the philosophical theories of phenomenology or hermeneutics to explore the effects of the dream on the humanities and social sciences.

Professor Krishnamurti decided to play devil's advocate for the group by announcing, "My aim is not some comfortable dialectical thesis but a total negation of everything expressed."

Professor Dussel, as a devotee of trans-modernism, was revitalized by a discourse that considered both tradition and modernity. The very nature of his approach emphasized spirituality when viewing things from the outside rather than the inside. He described it as an analogical way of thinking.

Professor Ketsela readily admitted that no African philosophical theory could address the magnitude of the topic before them. He subscribed to consensus after exhausting disjunctions that only dialogue could resolve. He insisted the group owed society an answer to the daunting question, Is the worldwide dream of harmonizing religion another unexplained phenomenon or a preemptive existential insight?

The forum would decide the next day.

Fr: Aliennus

To: Paraspermya

Via: Cosmic Telepathy

Re: Effects of the First Dream on Philosophers

Residual skepticism remains palpable concerning the source and meaning of the dream. As expected from the magnitude of such an anomaly, philosophic or religious adherents are loathed to accept any mysticism as truth.

Fr: Paraspermya

To: Aliennus

Via: Cosmic Telepathy

Re: Effects of the First Dream on Philosophers

Immediately convey to all philosophers the following expanded version of the first universal dream crafted in the Socratic logic that collates an unknown beginning with an unimaginable end.

A DREAM FOR PHILOSOPHERS

Soul is a condescending concept, ill-defined yet scintillating. But anxiety energizes life, leaving it to ego to defy the mystery of divine creation. Anxiety is fashioned by the dynamics of extreme stress. It's a streamlined universal energy that flows to overpower creativity, form, substance, and yes, even poetry. Soul is but the psychological and philosophical escape from it, sort of a musical interlude of life, evident from beginning to end and every moment in between. The center of nature from which Plato first split spirit from matter, and alchemy later disembodied from man only to be disavowed by Carl Jung, who preferred to juxtapose anxiety with spiritual consciousness.

Now the riddle ends! Universal forces are reconnected as extreme anxiety caused by stress was found to equal the displacement of dark matter, the only unified principle of the universe. Religious intolerance on Earth results in an overabundance of extreme cosmic stress, causing considerable discomfort in the universe by dislocating dark matter that can become existential to other celestial bodies. The solution is to restore religious peace on Earth by homogenizing religion or face eventual annihilation from a nearby black hole.

Upon reconvening the next day with the benefit of the highly focused second dream in mind, a roundtable discussion emerged. The professors revisited the philosophical need for religion in the first instance, and the need for people to kick the can down the road by praying when hope is lost. They resisted efforts to resolve the dilemmas themselves. The discourse was lively and sardonic but generally ran along the lines of the ancient poem that follows.

WHERE DO PRAYERS GO?

If you know how to worry, you know how to
pray, you know worrying gets you nowhere at all,
borrows future troubles—no more to say!

Anxious prayers can catch sinners who fall, but do they?
Prayers are old, new, about others, or you; some
are long, loud to be heard far away,

then there are silent prayers. Are they heard too?
Do prayers work this way? No one can say.

Eons ago, sinners and animals paid; sin was the fashion
served on a buffet, sacrifice assuaged, judgments
defrayed as Abraham offered his son as prey.

When atonement changed, civility trumped
brutality, prayer and sacrifice was exchanged,

Jesus died to end the barbarity.
Prayers, the new talisman, were just as damaged.

Pious illusions hid behind closed eyes, codified new
atonements for vice, avoided contrition, and risked
lies. Failure was high, answers not nice.

Reality to prayers is as truth is to wise. What
if life is no more than living erred?

The secret is out; the mystery dies.
All meet heaven at the beginning, not the end.

No more riddle; life is the test. Barter for praise, as
we pretend that poetic liturgy is a better end.

Thank God, I am an atheist!

Breaking News

Attending philosophers agree homogenizing religion can save the world from Armageddon. Religions that were built on egalitarian principles lasted a flickering moment and are now threatening human extinction by fighting and killing among themselves for prominence. They no longer serve mankind.

Fr: Aliennus

To: Paraspermya

Via: Cosmic Telepathy

Dream coda and an ancient poem both culled from Paraspermya combine to endorse homogenizing religion as a philosophy to contravene the hypocrisy of blind faith, unique to earthlings, not because of justifying imagined miracles by mass murder and maiming, but for the absence of an alternate rage against human suffering. The galactic dream awakened humanity to recoil at religious platitudes intended to thwart all truth or make it less bitter. Finally, the violence of religious wars has hollowed out humanity. The dream awakened them to the futility of murder as a sacrifice for righteous notions or atonement for fanaticism that threatens survival of the species. Religious justifications are now tenuous, and the cosmic consequences of pain and suffering became certainties. Still, clergies see heaven, and their crusaders see hell.

SCIENTIA TECHNIQUE

A FORUM OF SCIENTISTS

The internet, originally designed for scientists to share their findings with peers, lit up with ad hoc theories concerning the remarkably pervasive singular dream. The scientific community was concerned that apprehending this revelation could cause ordinary people to access a social universe without rules, and individual conduct could be as unique as a dream.

A forum of scientists gathered at the Royal Academy of Canada in Ottawa to question, distill, and provide evidentiary answers for this phenomenon. The attendees and their specializations included Stuart Hawking of the USA—gravity, cosmology, and radiation; Alexei Starobinsky of Russia—astrophysics and cosmology; Mikio Yamamoto of Japan—radiation and atomic physics; Malaf Al Mostakbal of Egypt—futurist; and Joseph Black of Scotland, UK—calorimetry.

The closest parallel to planet-wide events was light emanating from the sun, providing all energy to the world's ecosystem. The primary focus of the investigation by the scientists was narrowed to a new biological system of spatial variation. Like heat and temperature affect the biodiversity of poikilotherms and homeotherms, cold- and warm-blooded animals, the blanket dream is limited to humans—the only organism capable of laughing, evaluating, assimilating, and imparting its content through inorganic fixation. The prevailing view was that only a systematic approach would eventually explain the dilemma, not unlike the development of the indirect calorimeter that calculates the heat of living organisms by multiple regressions of their oxygen consumption. Proving the dream anomaly, rather than relying on mankind's need to glean miracles from unexplained phenomena, remained their challenge.

Once satisfied, Scientia Technique would conclude the debate and issue a finding the next day.

Fr: Aliennus

To: Paraspermya

Via: Cosmic Telepathy Re: Earth Science

Be advised the scientific approach to advanced reasoning mandates replication (usually lab controlled) of theories advanced by anomalies accompanied by debates and includes typical human competition for recognition.

Fr: Paraspermya

To: Aliennus

Via: Cosmic Telepathy Re: Earth Science

The challenge is both surprising and encouraging. Convey a highly focused second dream to all Earth scientists.

DREAM CODA FOR SCIENTISTS

It is axiomatic that science represents the world as it is proven, and religion represents it as each person would like to have it. People are easily deceived but very hard to undeceive as a continuum of wars prove. The solution to religious wars remains elusive after two millennia and now requires external persuasion, perhaps by a nonhuman authority!

Five scientific, earthbound experts of world renown shared the Nobel Prize in Science for proving an overload of extreme stress caused by religious wars is dislocating otherwise dark matter in the universe, which, in the short-term, causes global warming. In the long-term, humanity will vanish from the earth, one way or another, with no evolutionary descendants. If anyone happened to find themselves in a first-person dream experience, their dream was hijacked to experience a virtual recreation of how to prevent extinction by homogenizing religion now. Your expertise should be used to test or reproduce that anomaly by changing the laws of physics as you know them. Generate numerical models to track nuclear particles, as in lattice quantum chromodynamics, and model other anomalies to prove your theories. This one happens to be that collective dream designed directly to intervene in your state of consciousness, thereby simulating advanced reasoning required for unconditionally endorsing homogenizing religion.

Press Release

Scientia Technique, an international organization of theoretical and applied sciences, finds a permanent need to eradicate wars caused by religious differences. "These brutal hostilities to people also pollute the universe with inordinate extreme stress, possibly dislocating dark matter with a yin-yang effect, causing a cosmic imbalance of existential import. We, therefore, tacitly endorse homogenizing religion as we continue to research the religious genome."

THE UNITED NATIONS

THE ORGANIZATION

Over the millennia, mankind has, in good faith, crafted many instruments to avoid wars between and among nation-states. These stratagems included bilateral treaties, memos of understanding, regional tribunals, and international agreements. Special care was taken to permanently bind nations despite the transitory nature of governments, dominant tribes, religions, and races. The success of these attempts was spotty at best.

Hovering over these compelling arrangements, in addition to the entities involved, was the international organization of the United Nations (UN), whose function of legitimacy was recognized by 99 percent of the world's population, American Republicans notwithstanding. The UN was a forum that worked to resolve disputes among nations in a peaceful manner and avoid catastrophic wars. Their charter consisted of three tiers of reasonable stasis in addition to arbitrary veto power of a few privileged nations. These were the five permanent members of the Security Council, each of whom was a nuclear power. Their right of veto protected all other member states from a rogue nation declaring war against a nuclear power.

The secretary-general convened a plenary session of the General Assembly tier to determine if the unique dream experienced by every living human being on the same day was a hoax or a threat to the existing world order.

In the assembly, each ambassador to the UN opined for their country, after which the benefits of homogenizing religion became evident to the international body. Also evident was the improbability of 7 billion people abandoning ancient tenets of their religion imbedded into their DNA.

The plenary session adjourned until the next day.

Fr: Aliennus

To: Paraspermya

Via: Cosmic Telepathy

Subject: Diplomatic Skepticism

The United Nations is inclined to accept homogenizing religion as a new fact of life but is uncertain about how to approach their sovereign governments about it.

Fr: Paraspermya

To: Aliennus

Via: Cosmic Telepathy

Subject: Diplomatic Skepticism

Diplomats depend upon transient governments for their largess, arguing whatever cause is convenient for the day. Left to their own devices, they are often without an opinion. They will be subjected to a specialized dream for diplomats. When combined with the original dream for all mankind, they will be armed with valuable and verifiable facts to help move homogenizing religion forward to a reality.

DREAM CODA FOR DIPLOMATS

The UN is the largest herd ever assembled on Earth to deal with threats to peace and still play an integral role in fostering human rights and world health. However, you are held hostage to the sins of your forefathers, whose voices reverberate in your chamber with imperceptions of their own beliefs and misinterpretations of everyone else's. Their imprimaturs scour your mind of learned behavior with the extreme stresses and anxieties of their forebearers. Added to this, merciless observation of worldwide mental illnesses and modern-day hostilities show that your world is awash with an intergenerational hostile energy force radiating into a well-organized universe. For every action there is a reaction evidenced by depletion of your ozone layer of protection, the Van Allen radiation belts, and global warming. All this is caused by torrents of man-made negative ions of extreme stress and anxiety caused by the constancy of wars going on someplace on Earth, as ancient poets transcribed for Paraspermya. This is that translation.

FRACTURED PRISMS OF HUMANITY

Refracted lights allow us to see

the spectrum that colors self-righteousness with certainty.

So it is with moral conflicts
that begin with a certain clarity,

yet belies the underside of destruction and pity,
both last refuges of piety,

wars of certainty since creativity,
end in despoliation followed by bereavement,
generation after generation.

American history records twenty-seven wars
since 776,

and twenty smaller conflicts in-between.
Casualties were 3.2 million soldiers, most of them in teens.

Nine generations of young lost forever
to mad hypnotism of war's prisms.

The spectrum of war's colors is stained "dread"
since the fourth quarter of the eighteenth century,
when Revolutionary and Indian Wars left forty thousand dead.

The nineteenth-century color was vermillion,
for the War of 1812, Civil, and Spanish-American Wars
lost America another million.

Victories attained in the twentieth century were
many but bloodstained:

WWI, WWII, Korea, Vietnam, the Persian Gulf,
and twenty-six other minor conflicts

cost us the lives of another two million young conscripts.

Now here in the twenty-first, a century later,
sometimes we're the hated, not the hater,
still fighting monsters, but have we become one too?
Iraq, Afghanistan, this century's quid pro quo,
with thousands more casualties to date
and only eighty-six years left to go!

THE VOTE

The next day, the secretary-general initiated a proceeding before the Security Council, under Article 99, to recognize religious wars as a primary threat to international peace. Only the Security Council was empowered to determine the existence of such a threat and take actions to remedy it, under Articles 41 and 42. The council, not individual member states, was the sole arbiter under the UN Charter, empowered to call upon, order, or recommend compliance to the General Assembly. Toward this threat, Article 310 was added to the UN Charter, endorsing religious homogeneity to end wars and assure international peace.

The voting in favor of homogenizing religion was unanimous, and all ambassadors prepared to return home to convince their respective governments they no longer needed to trust in God.

ECONOMICS FOR
HARMONIZING RELIGION

THE ECONOMIC CHALLENGES FOR CLERICS

"This is Dr. Herbert Bernard of Worldwide PBS reporting from Davos, Switzerland, where I am about to interview several powerhouses on the economy of the world. Seated with me are Dr. U. S. Zellin, chair of the Federal Reserve Bank, of the US; Christmas LaGorgal Esquire, president of IMF Fund, of France; Dr. Gang Yi, vice chairman of the Bank of China, of China; Dr. M. L. Siregar, minister of finance, of Indonesia; and Professor William Vickrey, Nobel laureate in economics, of the US. Today, we will talk about the long-term effects homogenizing religion will have on world economics."

2014 UN Census Economic Fact Sheet
All Amounts Are US Dollars

1. Total Religious Adults Worldwide..................................$5 Billion
2. Global GDP...$80 Trillion
3. Worldwide Religion-Related Assets.............................$90 Billion
4. Annual Religious Contributions and Revenues.......$35 Billion
5. Net Worth of Global Religious Institutions.................$60 Billion
6. Excess Revenues (Annual, Tax-Free)...........................$6 Billion
7. Global Military Expenditures (Annual).....................$2 Trillion

The resulting discussion did not bode well for homogenizing religion. Almost 60 percent of the world's adults claimed to be religious adherents, and their impact on the global economy was gigantic. They decided that homogenizing religion could severely dislocate the world economic order. Religious tax-exempt contributions, as they were known, would likely disappear.

Worldwide religion-related assets (WRRA) would have to be liquidated or revamped for civil use. The net worth of global religious institutions would likely be substantially depleted, except reserves for pending pedophile litigation. As revenues dissolved, unemployed eleemosynars and clerics would increase in the absence of administering to 4,200 religions.

Fr: Aliennus

To: Paraspermya

Via: Cosmic Telepathy

Subject: Man-Made Economics

Please review these economic stipulations and challenges emanating from homogenizing religion and advise how to proceed to assuage them.

Fr: Paraspermya

To: Aliennus

Via: Cosmic Telepathy

Subject: Man-Made Economics

Impute the explanatory dream coda to every economist.

DREAM CODA FOR ECONOMISTS

From ancient tribal customs to modern-day superpowers, man-made economic systems favored property rights over human rights. Because of this imbalance that favored minorities and burdened majorities, the masses turned to religion for comfort and hope while the privileged property owners accumulated and marshaled worldly possessions to pass from generation to generation. They had no economic need for religion. Various cultures fashioned their own form of religious promises and threats to perpetuate adherents from generation to generation. And religious wars never proved who was right, only who was left. A few relatively influential souls were tacitly encouraged, actively financed, and then profited from these conflicts as they would from an insurance policy against anarchy. There was always a risk to their largess.

As the imbalance grew wider, religious wars became more frequent and more obscene. What is overlooked is these recurring wars are on just one planet, itself subject to universal laws in which mankind has no standing. These natural laws emanate from an absolute, universal balance of universal extreme stress and dark matter, each one an antagonist of the other. The abundance of fractious religious wars caused by flawed man-made economic systems birthed disharmony in the world and the cosmic balance, both of which must be restored to equilibrium.

Homogenizing religions is the only peaceful solution for ending these wars, reducing the extreme stress and anxiety of all people and rebalancing macroeconomic systems by earmarking religious assets and their supporting cash flows for a new university for homogenizing religion wherein the clergy is free to teach ancient religions during the millennium, and thereafter restore equanimity to the cosmic balance, from which a comprehensive economic science emerges.

CONCLUSION OF THE SYNOD

The coalition of economic experts at Davos unanimously agreed that homogenizing religion would obsolete war, restore world peace, and birth a new architecture for managing worldly resources that elevates human living standards, beginning with the US Affordable Care Act that adheres to the little understood yet incomparable cosmic-based economic dynamics. While all man-made economic systems were equal in import to indigenous laws, politics, and cultures, they were mutually exclusive in their applicability, humanity, and variety, each specifically designed to service democracy, capitalism, communism, feudalism, socialism, fascism, barterism, and many other isms. Homogenizing religion unleashed vast assets to enhance all forms of social governance.

THE SUPREME
MILITARY ALLIANCE

THE POETRY OF MONUMENTS

Generals sit erect atop monuments
while marble horses rear high.

Fallen comrades lie etched beneath.
Wartime presidents in chiseled rocks,
a bodiless soldier lies entombed,
wrapped daily in a fresh wreath.

Obelisks soar, marking feats of heroism,
granite arches harbor battles won and lost.

Uniform gravestones hide the dead from vandals,
iconic landmarks that stand in sun and frost.

Yet end comes to stones and the names thereon
as mountains wear, glaciers melt, and trees die,
nature mocking man's monolith phenomenon
to defy mortality gone awry.

Barbarism cut into weathered rocks,
a refuge for bloodstained swords not of a cynic,
cloaked by swarming pigeons

that come in flocks to edifices that are metaphoric.

We see enemies forward and aft,
But wars don't decide who is right,
only who is left!

This poem, "Monuments," was the commanding general's theme at the Supreme Military Alliance, held at the Imperial Hotel of Tokyo, to discuss the effect of harmonizing religion on future wars. He said, "No more wars? No more valor? Peace on earth? These are mere euphemisms for mothballing armaments and downsizing the military. Spending 2 trillion US dollars annually buys the world lots of killing machines and specially trained soldiers to maim, kill, and destroy society's citizens and property. The rest of the world combined doesn't spend as much. The military-industrial complex is an intricate, profitable, and vast global cartel, which drives the prosperity of every nation-state while they battle each other for superior religious and ideological preferences. Occasionally land and sea incursions cause local skirmishes, but wholesale religious wars dominate, by far. Homogenizing religion is anathema to our propaganda declaring a dominant military is the only hope for an enduring peace."

Everybody agreed to sleep on it and reconvene the following day.

Fr: Aliennus

To: Paraspermya

Via: Cosmic Telepathy

Re: Earth's Military Society

As expected, Earth's military-industrial complex selfishly guards its ever-growing dominance and perks in the world. They understand that homogenizing religion is an existential threat to their power base with no regard to its universal necessity. Any further dreams should emphasize that history is no assurance of the future.

Fr: Paraspermya

To: Aliennus

Via: Cosmic Telepathy

Re: Earth's Military Society

Agreed, convey a coda dream to the military.

DREAM CODA FOR THE MILITARY

Fueled by religious conflicts, regional wars seem to advance through similar stages. For example, during late antiquity of 400–800 BC, tribal squabbles between Christians, Islamists, and even secularists advanced into a conflagration between two-country kingdoms. Military strategy transformed slender hulled, oared galleys, powered by fifty rowers, used to transport tribal warriors to and fro into cast bronze rammers to strike and sink combatant ships, thereby escalating religious conflicts into open-sea wars. Bigger ships were soon needed for bigger rams that drove the need for more power rowers and larger crews. By the third century BC, Ptolemy IV built a behemoth to house three thousand sailors and four thousand rowers. A nautical absurdity evolved from religious squabbles. Fast-forward to the superpower Cold War that escalated geometrically until it ended, bankrupting the adversary, not concerned with religious or spiritual matters.

Since then, religious factions bent on destruction of all others circumvented the best and most expensive military strengths of developed nation-states. Weapons that are more intelligent lack enough defensive barriers to creative thinking. Consequently, the most effective military attacks from radical religionists are no longer predictable, and the best armed and led military forces are subject to threats from a relatively few technically savvy, ideological, fanatic, religionists. Wars begin today for the same reasons as before, swell in size by traditional military strategies, and will likely end in the same way, only to be repeated again and again. Harmonizing religion is to conflict as war is to peace. This is the way of the world!

At the next day's plenary session, the commander ordered a discussion on the philosophy of war. The ensuing repartee quickly revealed a variety of philosophies to which no more than two attendees agreed. Nonetheless, a lively discussion was held. Establishing a religious influence on war arose from a Messianic eschatological strategy, describing victory as imposing a single faith on the vanquished by the victors. Another more fatalistic theme was cast as teleological, an all-or-nothing scheme of religious war that is ongoing until the end of the world! The range of religious notions that drove generals toward a specific philosophy and heavily influenced battle strategies had nothing to do with minimizing casualties or deaths of ordinary soldiers under their command. The influence of both dreams, however, changed the defective philosophies of war forever.

Press Release

The military chiefs of the United Nations expressed their unity in favor of harmonizing religion for the progress and advancement of human morals and civilization while always respecting the need for worldwide military readiness.

A COUNCIL ON LONGEVITY

THE TOLL OF RELIGIOUS WAR

Second Millennium

Century (AD)	War-Related Deaths
I–XII	53.1 million
XIII	41.0 million
XIV	20.0 million
XV	1.0 million
XVI	5.1 million
XVII	37.1 million
XVIII	1.9 million
XIX	40.0 million

Third Millennium

XX–MMXIII	173.0 million
Total	**372.2 million**

Wars are the most unnatural cause of death on the face of the earth. They kill soldiers as a direct result of battle and civilians by collateral damage or outright genocide. Wars also induced pandemics. According to researchers, all wars were driven by religious obsessions often disguised as politics.

The longevity forum, among other things, took note that war-related deaths in the twentieth/twenty-first century exceeded those of the second millennium. There are four participants on the Council on Longevity:

1. Ambassador Harriet Frances Laughter, National Labor Relations director and record holder for twenty years of peaceful collective bargaining forums
2. Honorable Carol O'Stenes Sr., Esq., labor law judge advocate of long-term, peaceful, collective bargaining agreements and opera friend of Ambassador Laughter
3. Kenneth G. Siegel, EE, distinguished inventor of the persimmon nanotube diode for long-term interstellar travel
4. A. R. Audrey Coen, interplanetary traveling pollster and the youngest editor of the Hubbell-Cohen Digital Cosmos Encyclopedia

The council found irrefutable evidence against continuing multiple religious paradigms, which was compelling. None of the advantages claimed by religions in the name of their respective deities were compliant with the need to stop religious wars and the resulting chaos and extreme stress they produced. Also, considered by the council was the deteriorating political climate of the world that began in the twenty-first century and was no longer the cohesion that bound mankind despite political disparities. Liberalism, once the defining goal of most nation-states (post-Soviet dissolution, democracy expanded to one hundred nation-states from thirty), for the purpose of promoting peace from religious and political wars, had abruptly reversed direction to the more contentious course of extreme nationalism and dictatorship, thereby placing the efficacy of self-governing the planet in dire jeopardy. They feared this course reversal came at a time when killing technology was best and sufficiently apocryphal for the world to murder itself.

DREAM CODA FOR THE COUNCIL ON LONGEVITY

Rationally confident, emotionally terrified, extreme stress are the common core of the universe, infusing lives from embryo to death. Ever present in all matter, it is the strand that governs creation. Religious wars, on the other hand, are spastic constrictors of living matter. They strain subatomic particles with elongation, distortion, compression, and elasticity, vexing causes of mankind's extreme stress from the big bang to the speed of light. Religious wars, although confined to earth, generate uncontrolled heat, death, anxiety, and atomic fission. They distort the perfect balance of cosmic extreme stresses and displacements, the antimatter to gravity, and counterforce to all positive energy. They are the only universal constant. Religious wars are the dark phenomenon of earth, leading to the ultimate demise of the phenomenon of man at the core of the cosmos. Homogenizing religion is the only solution to avoid such grave consequences, preserve everlasting peace, and restore equilibrium among the galaxies.

CONCLUSION OF THE COUNCIL

The Council on Longevity recognized that religion and the resulting politics were both obsessive and compulsive diseases, likely to result in ending civilization as we know it. We endorse homogenizing religion as the only solution for human existence.

Fr: Aliennus

To: Paraspermya

Via: Cosmic Telepathy

Having sensed a favored pattern from dissecting and reconstructing the already vetted statistics and examining all other irrefutable evidence, we imparted a dream coda to the members of the council of Earth's long-term thinkers. I am happy to report their complete compliance and total acceptance of homogenizing religion. No further follow-up is warranted.

SYNCRETISM AND THE
SECOND UNIVERSAL DREAM

SYNCRETISM

The concept of homogenizing religion was accepted in the first year as a progressive revelation to a generation of people, the first ever exposed to it. The theme of this evolution was attributed to ending of worldly biases in accordance with present-day enlightenment, which they agreed to accept until proven otherwise.

Psychologically, humanity was proud of the comfort of lifelong religious teachings and spiritual needs ascending to a higher level of unification from unquestioned absoluteness while still retaining its moral truths. Notions of almost tribal exclusivity to their respective deities now reflected a concept of equality to comport with other religions while age-old differences were attributed to limited knowledge, or interest, to deal with them. This new manifestation of oneness still provided for different personalities, perceptions of reality, and individual imagination best suited to any time and place to express them. A foundation of new spiritual maturity was born. On this eponymous date, the whole world received the same dream again with which to apprehend the future.

A SECOND UNIVERSAL DREAM

Today, upon the earth's 253rd rotation in the year 2114, world religions celebrate as though it was New Year's Eve on the Julian calendar and will hereafter be known as Joan's Day. You, the people, get it! Homogenizing religion is a progressive revelation of the social condition to reach a new level of humanity's spiritual capacity in over two millennia. Certain aspects of all religions are unquestioned, but most are relative; For example, all religions prescribe honesty and denounce thievery but differ concerning women's rights, abortion, gay marriages, etc. Focusing on resolving such differences can evolve into an even higher stage of unification. Think about them because that day has arrived!

Wars rarely result from such absolutes as homogenizing religion. Rather they are caused by misinterpreting religious rituals and archetypes. Another area to consider is that all religions profess the same spiritual and metaphysical nature, but they differ on who represents them to their faithful. Ancient intermediaries as Moses, Christ, Muhammad, etc. were well suited to appear and express them at a specific time and place according to the prevailing culture at the time. They were all purveyors of a singular truth. Different interpretations were made over centuries by observers, not what was being observed. Subsequently, these differences cascaded in the imagination and mythology of generations, to eventually evolve into unintended dogmatic beliefs.

Homogenizing religion rises above ideologies inherited from ancient causes of extreme stress and anxiety, the murder and maiming of at least 500 million people in the second millennium and dislocated the cosmic equilibrium between natural, extreme stress and its antithesis, the dark matter. Today, as you dream, the magnetic field of your sun is 230 percent stronger than before; the moon acquired an atmosphere of 6,000 km of natrium that wasn't there before. The polar ice and a new magnetic field are observed on Mercury. The aurora of Venus is brighter by 2,500 percent. The polar icecaps of Mars are disappearing, to be replaced by huge storms. The brightness of Jupiter's plasma clouds increased by 200 percent. Saturn's equatorial jet streams are disappearing. Uranus's clouds are unusually active. Neptune is 40 percent brighter; the atmosphere of Pluto is 300 percent heavier even as it recedes from the sun; Earth's axis is changing; plasma at the edge of your solar system has increased 1,000 percent. The hyperdimensional ethers and mass-less wave energies of the universe are growing more complex. All are a consequence of Earth's hyper-extreme stress caused by religious wars. A constitution of homogenizing religion combined with a single bible, or website, like the apocryphal Baha'i, can ease this ubiquitous but extreme stress on the universe by restoring peace and tranquility to Earth and throughout the cosmos.

This then constitutes the beginning of the rebirth of mankind—once submerged in an invisible sea of biased thoughts, ideas, and instructions, now bathed in a purposeful stream of wakefulness for its survival. The whole universe glows with cautious optimism for eternal peace. It's almost as though Earth is finally immersed in syncretic thoughts.

Fr: Aliennus

To: Paraspermya

Via: Cosmic Telepathy

Re: Syncretism and the Second Universal Dream

The second universal dream of the world was executed today with convincing transparency for the benefit of future generations on Earth as codified in the following manifesto for homogenizing religion.

EXISTENTIAL CHALLENGES TO HOMOGENIZED RELIGION

PREAMBLE

WHEREAS we, the civilized society of Earth, commit to respond as one to existential threats to humanity by renouncing the ubiquitous practice of violence to defend unrelenting, chaotic, and destructive religious laws, rules, archetypes, and traditions. While secular civil laws, the embodiment of an intellectual tradition of social philosophy that began with Socrates, steadily advanced, the staid dogmas of religion did nothing but frustrate the reality of human progress with rituals that bred religious wars, mass mental illness, and put extreme stress on the entire universe. This manifesto and its amendments codified morals proven to advance humanity despite past religious devastation.

SECTION I: DOCTRINES AND REALITY

Homogenizing religion harmonizes selected spiritual doctrines with reality.

The universality of the ten spiritual commandments was adopted as primary law for mankind. That doctrine, created in the first millennium, imposed moral imperatives that render most others moot. Numerous metaphysical abstractions merely developed mechanisms to identify conflicts among people, punish the offenders, and encourage violence. Left unchecked, these theological articles of faith aided and abetted the murder of millions of people and succeeded in upsetting the cosmic balance and threatened annihilation of the human species. The reality that emerged from harmonizing religion better integrates the intended but unachievable experiences of piety with humanity.

SECTION II: HUMAN SUFFERING

Homogenizing religion is not indifferent to human suffering.

Unlike extreme stress, an organic behavior evident throughout the universe, civilized behavior is gratifying and restorative for humans. However, unlike cosmic easing manifested by anti-matter, emotional suffering is optional for conscious minds and is as painful as if it were physical. Religionists relied on human suffering as justification for their own social status, offering consolation to the afflicted, whether by compassionate affirmation or damnation. This offering morphed into symbols of imagined callings to lead a prescribed holy life as penance. Homogenizing religion ascribes to a higher state of relief for human suffering than these pseudo-theological remedies.

SECTION III: DESPOTS

Homogenizing religion is of no use to despots.

Religious sentiments were a principal element in the rise of false messiahs over the ages. History abounds with wannabe world saviors who promised peace but failed to deliver it. Religions continuously conferred its aspects of divinity on delusional people, defining them as saviors, emperors, sovereigns, or living saints, and those sanctified endorsements endured for centuries. Fear from conjured religious discrimination created tyrants, who prosecuted pseudo-religious wars cascading over the millenniums. In all the forms of human governance, only despotism can govern by hallucinations and caprice rather than laws derived from nature and human needs.

SECTION IV: BETWEEN CONSCIOUSNESS AND META PHYSICALITY

Homogenizing religion respects the dichotomy between consciousness and the metaphysical.

When is the human mind immaterial? Only when compared to the laws of physics pertain to matter and not human emotions or feelings that are preprogrammed with specific intuitions concerning the body but not the mind. Both, however, combined to form the essence of human life on Earth— demonstrated by the use of free will exclusive to mankind, who is conscious of feelings and emotions, and the resulting physical acts. Whether one or the other is causative remains a mystery.

SECTION V: RIGHTS, PROPERTY, COMMERCE, AND SOCIETY

Homogenizing religion is animus to perpetuating a social human species.

The right to life in any society no longer depends on linking folklore with reality. Adherence to a religion increased poverty and barbarous acts. It tainted liberty and commerce; it is striking and provocative, and its touch points are preemptive elements for conflict. Faith must never be an acceptable substitute for real solutions to human problems, thereby abolishing the fodder for religious wars at the source.

SECTION VI: PROSELYTIZING

Homogenizing religion reduces the discordant preoccupation with proselytizing.

Human passions, whether innate, induced, or acquired, are not forcibly exportable to others. Also known as pioneering, witnessing, and evangelizing, proselytizing is an aggressive form of moral suasion couched in covert ethics and righteous wisdom. Renouncing one unnatural belief for another that claims everlasting life as an ultimate reward is the sole purpose for marshalling strength in other to prolong wars of natural attrition. During the past millennia, each religion in the world provoked violence at one time to perpetuate their own abstractive beliefs by herd psychosis.

SECTION VII: AFTERLIFE PROMISES

Homogenizing religion does not require prayers or sacrifices, human or animal, for promises of an afterlife of felicity and perfection.

Nothing escapes the universe regardless of mankind's incantations. The one absolute that revisionists miss is that everyone meets their maker at the beginning, not at the end, of life.

SECTION VIII: MIRACLES AND IMAGININGS

Homogenizing religion still encourages belief in miracles, visions, and extraordinary occurrences that emanate from real-time experiences.

Wisdom is an internal phosphorescence that amplifies human imagination, exaggerates the joy of thinking yet demands truth. Those who possess it experience small miracles from a ripened mix, especially if imagination and dreams produce conscious thoughts. The question is, Are dreams imagined or induced? Since they occur independent of reality, they never mingle, but they do leave imprints on the brain. Only humans dream, and while the dreams in no way imply a supernatural intervention, how then was the dream of homogenizing religion first realized, planned, and executed? The mystery continues. Perhaps the future will reveal the answer.

SECTION IX: UNIFYING CULTS

Homogenizing religion recognizes that human unification begins as cultish but ends encompassing singularity.

A paradox of past millennia is that warlike nation-states are more literate than gender-biased countries. From this conundrum, it can be discerned that education stokes competition, materialism, and greed while the lack thereof thrives, among other things, on misogyny. These extremes are traceable. Each is infused with religious justification to specifically focus on conflict among zealots controlling others.

However, homogenizing religion promotes peace among all people by advancing humanity.

SECTION X: TRANSPARENCY

Homogenizing religion is manifestly transparent.

Religious convictions enhance obsessive mystiques, and radical results often leading to violence. While homogenizing religion might not eradicate all diverse preferences, it tempers extremes and restores sanity, thereby avoiding the major cause of wars among people.

SECTION XI: SACRED MUSIC

Homogenizing religion favors forces of musical expressions replete with the harmonics of the cosmos and tuned to living.

The galactic universe pulses and vibrates with quasars, pulsars, star systems, and asteroids emitting their unique harmonics. On Earth, these notes are corralled by religionists of every persuasion, including counterculture anthems, songs, poems, chants, and hymnals. They are recognizable by their unique register, density, dynamics, texture, and timbre that mimic spatial sounds for all life-forms to elicit extraterrestrial endorsements for eleemosynary purposes.

SECTION XII: COSMIC RECOGNITION

Homogenizing religion is mankind's encounter with the cosmic membrane of cognition. The everlasting and only extraterrestrial contact ever.

Human evolution on Earth progressed from simple consciousness to an exclusive self-awareness, evidenced by thought, reason, and imagination. Too often, however, it was diluted by an inexplicable need to dominate by violence. This innate corruption severely reduced the time, effort, and treasure needed for advancing mankind's cognition even further. The gateway to improving human intellect is to combine intuition with uncovering facts, avoid wars of domination among 4,200 religions, and unite with the combined knowledge of a singular yet diversely stream of consciousness.

PART II

A CENTURY LATER

LIVING THE DREAM

One hundred years after Aliennus imparted the same dream to 7 billion people as they slept, it still resonated, but those who dreamt were all dead. Four generations later, humanity evolved into a contemplative civilization on successively higher planes from what once was a fractious religious society. Some found humor in the pursuit of homogenizing religion, as related on some news networks.

"Where would we be today if the legendary apocryphal dream was only a wet one?"

"Can you imagine changing from acting as a clerical intermediary between people and their gods to obsolete sages in just four generations?"

"Is homogenizing religion a reality or just a delusion with which everyone agrees?"

THE SOCIOECONOMIC IMPACT ON SOCIETY

Homogenizing religion had a collateral challenge, resulting in an essential need for society to research, study, and document the pure economic benefit or burden religion, organized or unorganized, had on civilization over two millennia or, at a minimum, during the second millennium.

The enormity and complexity of this endeavor so inspired academia that newly specified postgraduate degrees in the socioeconomic import of ancient religions were offered to student researchers. Their task was to locate and investigate heretofore hidden and secret records of eleemosynary entities showing monies, usually tax-free, garnered from faith-based businesses, philanthropies, gifts, and contributions, and how those funds were used for society at large. These included recompense, if any, for child abuse, fraud, passivity in face of human genocide, and funding violent extremisms that contributed to the wars and casualties referred to in the dream. This multigenerational project directly translated the mental and emotional landscape of ancient religions with all their dimensions and mechanisms into a cogent comprehension for third millennium scholars. Already known and codified by internationally accepted accounting principles was the nominal wealth of all 4,200 religions. This amount peaked at annual revenues of 4.5 trillion US dollars to support physical assets of 20 trillion US dollars. In the US alone, religious revenues peaked at 1.2 trillion US dollars, annually generated from physical assets of 8 trillion US dollars. Unlocking and releasing these measured economic forces into a society of homogenizing religion was a pursuit of an unknown beginning and an unimaginable end. There would be more of these visionary endeavors in the third millennium.

Ending religious wars and achieving enduring peace had a rocky start, but the challenges differed considerably. For example, ascribing Earth's bounty and mankind's treasure for organized murder to resolve religious disputes was replaced by an existential need for prosperity to feed a burgeoning global population, reaching 10.4 billion people. It began with reallocating religious assets to education and science. The University of Homogenizing Religion (UHR) established graduate schools for studying ancient religions wherever cathedrals, synagogues, temples mosques, and other houses of worship were situated. These specialized institutions taught core courses in all ancient religions, including their historical glory and gore, as well as their transition to world peace by assimilating into a homogenized religion. The faculty for UHR and its specialty schools consisted of intergenerational descendants of clerics qualified by motivation to teach a religion of choice, as well as tangible benefits of homogenized religion, to students and residual worshippers at chapel facsimiles situated on each campus.

UNINTENDED CONSEQUENCES

Homogenizing religion, while a major factor in providing life-sustaining services, was not enough. Other changes were essential companions for people to face a new reality. For example, potable water for continuous irrigation of an ever-expanding food supply was needed for human consumption. All this in the face of accelerated global warming that demanded acts thought to be beyond the scope of mankind's competence, and the risk was an unimaginable end. Solutions were urgently required.

One problem was readily solved by tethering a continental size calving of an ice cap glacier and storing it to meet mankind's long-term needs. It was transported by ocean tugs to the headwaters of the Colorado River to be eased into the Grand Canyon until filled and dammed to keep the Colorado River at flood stage forever. Infrastructure engineering could then distribute water as needed. Human ingenuity executed similar solutions worldwide, all within a century of experimenting with homogenizing religion. This was a good indication that humanity could be saved. As a result of religious peace, ingenious bioengineering, and life-extending medical sciences, mortality rates dropped precipitously and birth rates exploded, precipitating a crucial need for more efficient and expanded land use while faced with global warming and coastal submersion.

Demographics showed that the exponential need for potable water, irrigation, grazing, and human habitation required for an additional landmass of 25.5 million habitable square miles to satisfy the midmillennium population. Global warming accelerated in the twenty-first century submerging several million square miles of densely habituated continental coastlines, making reclamation essential as the contravening forces of population explosion and planet warming increased geometrically.

THE MOSES COMMISSION

Charlton Moses, a universally recognized master builder, was impressed into service by the UN to head a taskforce to reclaim submerged coastal landmasses, expropriate more land from the oceans, and tangentially explore the plausibility of rehabilitating uninhabitable deserts, mountains, and continental shelves, all to support the explosion of human life resulting from homogenizing religion a century ago.

His lineage as an architect and engineer was traceable to the Egyptian Imhotep, a creator of the Great Pyramid of Giza in the twenty-seventh century BC; brushed by Archimedes, a distant relative; and the Roman structural engineer Vitruvius. Moses approached big projects with ideas and images that could survive only in his mind. He really designed mental structures as opposed to physical ones. It was said that Moses climbed inside the psychology of huge projects.

Moses translated his ideas and mental structures into mathematical dimensions and mechanics, materials, and budgets for the outer parameters of yet an unknown physical application and was supported by a group of eight master engineers, each representing one continent. Of the 197 million square miles (MSM) of Earth's surface, water covered 71 percent (140 MSM), and 14 percent (28 MSM) was uninhabitable. Human life was currently supported by a shrinking 15 percent (29 MSM) of Earth's surface. The consequences of homogenizing religion in just one century became as daunting as the existential benefits. Humanity seemed to be entangled in a Gordian knot.

The UN headquartered Moses and his minions in a spacious, well-appointed mansion in Zug, Switzerland, tucked safely between the pyramids of the Alps and the European continental plains. They were accorded every convenience so as not to distract them from their world-saving mission. Once settled in, they brainstormed face-to-face in pairs, and in daily plenary sessions, which often lasted around the clock. All ideas were encouraged so long as their plausibility squared with state-of-the-art engineering sciences, and the somewhat radical ideas had to have at least a tenuous possibility of realization.

Addressing the elite group upon which the world awaited, Moses said, "We all know of the genius, albeit abstract, reason the dilemma of assuring the world of five hundred years of potable water and irrigation was created, planned, and developed. Until now, it was a work in process evolved from out-of-the-box thinking. Well, no less is expected from us. We are here to find all manner and ways to rehabilitate landmass enough to retain human and animal life for the next five hundred years. The greatest engineering feats ever known to mankind emerged from enveloping our necessity with inventive ideas." He went on, "I want to hear every morsel of your thinking, no matter how absurd you may think it, so let's begin to throw everything against the wall and see if something sticks!"

MEMBER PROPOSALS

"What I have to propose," said Master Engineer Emile Europa, "has as great philosophical consequences as the squeeze of overpopulation and landmass loss. For reconciling the need to survive and still preserve human dignity is at times conflicting."

"Please, go on," said Moses.

Europa continued, "Recognizing that more people are dead than alive and their final resting place occupies almost 5 million square miles worldwide of raw land, if cemeteries could be obliterated and new burials prohibited, possibly requiring cremations, we can reclaim as much as 10 percent of our landmass goal within twenty years at a cost of 20 trillion dollars while providing work for 25 million laborers."

Moses pondered the first effort put forth, stroked his beard, and said, "After experiencing homogenizing religion, to eradicate the one remaining sacred event is likely to elicit widespread emotional resistance from descendants and cast aspersions on the value of a purely physical existence. However, the suggestion is palpable but requires careful public-relation preparations in the absence of a convincing universal dream."

Europa, who suffers no fool's errand, replied, "Fortunately random event generators [REGs] that also influence human consciousness and reaction have been in place since the twenty-first century when the population was alert to terrorists. These REGs interface with computers in over one hundred thousand locations worldwide, creating a database of synchronized sequential reactions to disturbances that is better than relying on trends for the markedly human herd mentality. Programmed to convince society that trading a cemetery-free society for alkaline hydrolysis, they can contribute to ending the crisis and extending human existence. We should see results faster than our ancestors, who adopted homogenized religion a century ago. They witnessed the extreme stress emanating from religious wars that dispersed among the cosmos, and they were present when it was reduced by an anomalous yet instructive dream that explained the import of restoring equanimity to dark matter. Now we are faced with the consequences of homogenizing religion, overstressing the galaxies and restricting star production. The problem is equally existential and requires us to act."

The theory of creation had, by this time, evolved from earlier theories of the big bang or intelligent creation to one in which the universe resulted from an ejection of matter from the mother of all black holes and the coalescing of DNA, RNA, and other biotics to form Earth. It then left the rest to fill the universe with the detritus of star-birthing materials—what was called galaxies, which was suspended in dark matter to be traversed only by Paraspermya—the residue of the one and only human species. The success of Aliennus's mission was now in the hands of Moses and the continentals. How to influence them sublimely, however, was still within his province.

Duncan D'nunda was an engineering genius who made his reputation by irrigating the Australian Outback. He rerouted the slipstream from the continent's eastern rain forest for over twenty-five years when everyone thought it a fool's errand.

D'nunda began to speak, "Some of my best results began with thinking outside the box. At first blush, my colleagues and potential clients always think I'm a bit of a 'roo from down under, as I am sure you folks will. Just hear me out, think about the solution I am suggesting, and let it percolate overnight. Many great things emerge the next morning from a good night's sleep, as you all know."

He continued, "Advances in laser technology is so profound that we can virtually exercise the similar control of space, weather, oceanography, and terrain that nature can. Recent beta projects conducted by the International Space Agency [ISA], Ocean and Atmospheric Consortium [OAC], and the Geo-Environmental Group [GEG] of the UN succeeded in drilling down to the earth's mantle at the Marianas Trench in the Pacific Ocean, cutting a one-square-mile swath of mantle from the International Space Station Laser Laboratory [ISLL]. This effort was closely correlated with the latest and largest 3D printer housed on a reconstituted ancient oil rig anchored over the drill site. The 3D printer fabricated and installed a high-tension, heat-resistant trench shoring material that withstood the deepest water pressure on the planet, which the Marianas Trench is known for, and was impervious to the intense heat arising from the earth's core through its mantle. It worked!"

Moses and his group was mesmerized by D'nunda, who paused to hydrate his throat with bottled water and continued, "Ocean water poured into the newly cut trench at a rate of 25 million gallons per minute and evaporated at the same rate, producing high-pressure steam that rapidly rose fifteen miles into the stratosphere, seeding the jet stream as it flew by to produce voluminous and continuous rain that irrigated the deserts in its wake. Therefore, ten thousand square miles of submerged land was recovered near Guam and the Marianas archipelago. The reignited fertility of the Great Desert of the outback restored another seventeen thousand square miles for repopulation."

The Australian engineer concluded, "I estimate by expanding the ISLL to six extreme lasers, we can recover 8 million square miles of submerged coastal land and reclaim 10 million square miles of Earth's deserts, at a cost of 100 trillion US dollars spent over a century. This reclamation project would also prevent further land erosion of approximately 13 million square miles, or one-half, of our need for the next 250 years."

Moses was duly impressed with the out-of-the-box thinking and uttered to the group, "We just conceptualized about 70 percent of our mission after hearing from just two participants. Way to go!"

Ms. Frances Sogi, DSc, a world-renowned big project engineer of Japanese-Caucasian descent, was chosen to represent the Asian continent in Moses's minion. She trained at MIT in America, the Max Plank Institute in Europe, and Beijing University of Space Engineering in China. She also conceived, designed, consulted, and managed huge engineering projects for the UN, from erecting dams to removing and reconstructing coastal cities threatened by global warming. Her approach to these major projects was avant-garde at the time but well-grounded in engineering science and particularly noteworthy for pushing people beyond their limits to understand complicated concepts, subsequently establishing new standards. She was often compared to the legendary architect Frank Lloyd Wright of twentieth-century fame.

She began to speak, and the group fell silent. "At best, our mission is the most complex ever, save human reproduction, and at worst, humanity depends on us to save them and possibly the million other species that inhabit Earth. That's a pretty big matzo ball hanging out there."

Moses knew he asked for extreme ideas from his brilliant delegates and already experienced a couple of those. He instinctively expected hers to be as well.

Dr. Sogi continued to expound on her purview. "We heard from Emile how far laser technology has advanced, and I can add so have the uses to which laser technology can be adapted when enhanced by wireless apps. It is in this vain that I conceived a method by which we can restore 10 million square miles of uninhabitable surface for habitation. My plan, in a nutshell, is to reverse mankind's obsession to climb mountains, trying but rarely reaching summits, and bring the mountains of the world down to us by cutting down most mountain ranges to sea level, leaving Machu Picchu in the Andes. We will simultaneously build up their contiguous valleys to sea level with mountainous detritus, thereby increasing our Earth's life sustaining surface by 50 percent. We possess the technology to do that," she emphasized.

The delegates visualized cutting down the Himalayas, filling its contiguous valleys, which all mountains have, into a level plain at sea level that can support agriculture and reservoirs. In addition, the solid rock foundations will enable skyscrapers and vast cities to be built for the first time in history. They thought it was extreme but wondered how it would be done.

Dr. Sogi continued, "Our reconstruction platform will incorporate ISLL, and secure a wireless remote control of geostatic nuclear fueled extreme laser drones [ELD] to hover around each selected mountain until the predetermined cutting bias is level with the surrounding valleys before moving on to the next mountain in the range. The ISLL can manage up to five hundred ELD squadrons simultaneously assigned throughout the world. I estimate a worldwide completion date of two hundred years at a cost of 150 trillion US dollars."

Following a collective sigh, Moses adjourned the meeting until the next day. As each member of the team returned to their private quarters to prepare for the next day's brainstorming session, Aliennus struck again on the one-hundred-year anniversary of homogenizing religion.

DREAM CODA FOR THE
MOSES COMMISSION

While in REM sleep, each engineer dreamt of their great-great-grandparents, who experienced the original dream of homogenizing religion to save the planet and whose wisdom passed to their generational offspring concerning the anomaly that caused them to act to end murders provoked by religious wars. Their ancestors passed on their knowledge of the consequences of excessive strains from continuous killing that rocked the cosmos with regularity and force as to finally displace the very galactic glue of dark matter that mitigated the stresses and strains of existence on other universes. That is, atavistically explaining, how the world woke from a common dream, worked to find common ground among 4,200 religions, and finally embraced homogenizing religion and lived to see the end of religious wars. But in the haste toward fulfilling the promise of everlasting peace, unintended consequences were spawned. These were experienced by their great-great-grandchildren, who were tasked to remedy them as they dreamt like their ancestors once did a hundred years before them.

We are proud that our bloodlines run in your veins and fuel your dedication to the task at hand, which rose inadvertently from our dream of homogenizing religion a hundred years ago. In tackling the presence of an enormous problem of overpopulation with the skills and extreme technologies it deserves, at least for a short-term solution, you and your colleagues are to be praised. However, you know too well that earthborn advances in technology, while impressive, are inherently prone to obsolescence. The nature of this project and the real solution, however, is existential and therefore long term. We, your ancient ancestors, take ownership of causing the excess of humanity with which you must now cope and will guide you toward a more permanent solution. One that can be likened to an interactive museum, engineered by caring curators, displaying people's needs when living in a seasonal environment with subterranean water and plains that comprise 40 percent of the landmass, a silicate mantle that prevents quake-like tectonic plate movements, more commonly known as earthquakes, and erupting volcanoes. Soil nutrients, when reconstituted, were comparable to the mother planet Earth. So you see, we are not talking about staying on Earth, and yes, you are urged to populate Mars!

With the excess population caused by homogenizing religion forever eradicating earthen wars a century ago, emigration from the host planet should be voluntary and continuous after identifying and qualifying interplanetary immigrants as bona fide progeny of once warlike casualties of religious hostilities now banished by homogenizing religion. The methods are up to your free will to decide. Mars is one-half the diameter of Earth but equal in landmass with no surface water as yet. The rate at which humans age on Mars is twice as fast as Earth, and so a long-term migration stream is essential to maximize the occupation by humanity. I am giving you a heads-up for the need of a synthetically controlled inner atmosphere in the absence of any, but your recent breakthrough in chemically converting sand

*to energy provides the unlimited indigenous power
needed for almost any planetary purpose.*

*Your REM sleep is almost at an end, and you will
awake at rest, recognizing the long-term engineering
solution to your world's existential dilemma.*

The next day, Moses reconvened the forum by announcing what
he thought was his own daunting dream. He quickly learned his
engineering group dreamt the same dream at the same time. Their
collective disbelief mirrored the same reaction of their ancestors'
a hundred years earlier, but this time, with smiles of satisfaction
for experiencing first-hand an opinion from an outlier. Faced with
deciding on a course to preserve humanity, Moses searched for the
wisdom of Solomon by brainstorming his Mensa-like council of
experts. They ran and reran the numbers to test the plausibility of
each possibility, reconstituted each theory for weeks, all to no avail.
He and his elite group knew that a consensus would have great
weight with the UN General Assembly to whom they reported.
Any recommendation made by them with less than unanimous
agreement would merely kick back the problem to the UN and
further delay the need to slow down depleting the resources of the
planet. The solutions presented by Doctors D'nunda and Sogi, along
with the outlier's dream coda, exceeded the minimum expectations
for job creation, technological plausibility, social acceptability,
feasibility, and risk/reward analysis. Solving the overwhelming
economic costs was another matter.

The multigenerational effort required for each proposed solution
constituted lifestyle changes, diluting traditional cultures, and
reallocating global assets with no guarantee of success—just a
possibility. With such vast stakes at hand, Moses felt overwhelmed.
Nonetheless, the world awaited his recommendations with bated
breath, as attested to by daily press conferences to track progress.

Finally, Moses completed the report of his findings to the UN, the only organizational body capable of deciding the fate of the world. His conclusion was prominently displayed coincident with the filing of his report.

THE COMMISSION'S FINAL RECOMMENDATIONS

The Moses Commission, after twenty-five years work, recommends the following solutions, in Aristotelian sequence, to save mankind from the heretofore unintended consequences of homogenizing religion. We conclude the feasibility report be offered as a referendum to the generation of its time to decide on the best path for survival of future generations. We offer the following five options: reversed interment, land/sea reclamation, recontouring mountains, emigration to Mars, and harnessing fulminology.

The infinite scope of this project is beyond any other one undertaken on Earth in the history of humankind, including the theory of evolution, upon which we still rely to explain all universal events. Consequently, the paradigm adopted ranged from certitude to plausible imagining. The reality of the projected breadth, length of time, or depth of required knowledge were regarded with the same reverence for wandering imaginings, restrained only by the bounds of truth. Once an idea qualified for further consideration, however, the methodology employed subjected it to a gauntlet of tests for perception and conceptual cognition, both ranked by the unproven likelihood of success. There was a need to create new knowledge after such leaps of sensory perception, so outside-the-box thinking was crafted into theories, plans, policies, and measures reflective of the mission.

THE CENTENNIAL
CELEBRANTS

DOME OF THE ROCK

Remnant members of what once was the Reverential Guild of Scholars of Ancient Religions met at the meticulously maintained Dome of the Rock, an artifact of ancient religions, now leased to the university's specialty school for the centennial celebration. Guests included faux clerical clergy who were fourth generation teachers/actors with a flair for Shakespearean rhetoric and descendants of scholars who participated in the original debate on homogenizing religion. No biological descendants of Pope Luke II were present.

Opening day included an abundance of favorite foods of the ancients, such as pastrami, couscous, dates, nuts, caviar, vodka, matzo, rice, and beans, to infuse the atmosphere with authenticity. The ensuing feast was followed by a plenary discussion of core teachings of homogenizing religion that began in the twenty-first century. It was noted that student admissions increased steadily for courses in ancient religions practiced up to and including the twentieth century sans interest in their ancient myths, rituals, and archetypes. There was also no interest in the architecture of their houses of worship, now converted to classrooms, the interiors of which were facsimiles of those very temples and churches. Long ago, the regents agreed that electives in religious rituals and practices would suffice. After all, participation in creating a charter of homogenizing religion, where a unitary bible was the preferred curriculum of students and faculty requiring more room for further development. The agenda for the next day reserved time for lectures space the scholarly celebrants to exchange ideas.

Meanwhile, the Union of Universal Philosophers and the International Academy of Sciences convened at the Royal Victoria Hotel in Montevideo, a preferred venue for world-renowned philosophers, as it was a century ago. They were joined by a new generation of tenderfoot philosophers and scientists, who were mesmerized by three-dimensional interactive posters and streaming videos of the original gathering in the vast hotel lobby for all to see and marvel at. An imposing thematic banner flashed neon lights that read, "Harmonizing religion is not just another unexplained phenomenon for us homeotherms!"

It was acknowledged that the global, profession-specific dreams of a century ago remained a mystery, philosophically speaking. It was known, however, that they enlightened and transformed cynical ideologies of a herd of single-minded religionists. In a single century, an entire millennium of 4,200 individual religions that produced more casualties by polarization than any other human endeavor was transformed into the nirvana of homogenized religion, unheard of in any annals of philosophy or scientific history up to that point. Human thoughts and beliefs once hidden behind religious walls of a pseudoscience of fanatical imaginings that created human brutality opened up to the cure for which was more threatening to self-righteous religionists than the problems they bred.

Only one hundred years later, it seemed anything was possible. Humans and financial resources were devoted to social needs in the absence of any war preparations, and although originally thought to be far-fetched, imaginative ideas to feed an ever-expanding human population became reality. Fertile fields emerged from deserts when liberally irrigated with glacial waters siphoned from natural basins and land depressions. Once freed by a common dream from the stress of designer killing, mankind focused on construction, not destruction. While much remained to be done to assure the tranquility of future generation, it appeared that Armageddon was cheated, but maybe it wasn't.

Physical results were obviously enjoyed by all, but emotional conflicts remained camouflaged from generation to generation, proving to be an ever-present challenge. Old habits die hard, particularly when used as a tether to bind families together on the same level as DNA. Unexplained rituals, beliefs, and archetypes with spooky notions fester below the surface despite the easy acceptance of homogenized religion as dogma. Such restlessness slows progress to a snail's pace and is apathetic and time consuming to overcome. Centuries-old traditions simmered below the surface. Universal dreams worked, but subcutaneous leaching of "once upon a time" antics survived.

Four generations passed since the effects of Aliennus's mission inspired humanity to follow a dream for 36,500 days! Whatever misgivings they harbored, not once over four generations had anyone outright refused to partake in homogenized religion. It's was akin to the ghost of Hamlet revisiting to sing encomiums of the string theory to us—unless, of course, we rewrite history to presume it our discovery.

Invisibility and denial was part of the allure since it was easier for the people of the world to ignore what they didn't want to see. It's as if human cognition had a perception filter hard-wired to their brains. In the earthly experience, invisibility was tantamount to impunity, so surreptitious corruption was liberated from all obligations of decency. It was such an insidious form of power that, in fact or fiction, no one became invisible without an ulterior motive. Once chosen, invisibility transformed into a superpower. Once forced upon them, it became a plight on all humanity. The closest they came without plunging into it was a clever camouflage similar to that adapted by animal predators and their prey, and they were not always successful. Yet invisibility was all around. Physicists estimated that only 5 percent of the universe was visible. Science proved that humans see almost nothing that is hostile to them, like germs, viruses, genes, ocean depths, and atmospheric heights that lack oxygen. They even taught their children that what is unseen or kinetic is what counts most in the quality of life. How, then, did they know if they chose a course of self-destruction from an unseen entity or discovered one on their own?

UNITED NATIONS
OF THE FUTURE

THE UNITED NATIONS

The United Nations, having long since established itself as the premier international organization of nation-states rather than individuals, companies, or agencies, was expected to discuss, debate, and vote on the existential consequences of homogenized religion and the referendum results as reported by the Moses Commission. The environment in which the UN operated was among the most privileged. It was insulated from peeping Toms, reporters, pollsters, and investigators, except by invitation. Functioning as such for a century, it evolved into a diplomat's haven for social intercourse among member diplomats. All others were outliers.

The UN global edifice located in New York City, USA, grew exponentially on land donated by ancient Rockefeller scions and encompassed Governors Island on the east, Seventy-Ninth Street on the north, and Madison Avenue on the west, displacing small businesses and numerous low-cost residences in its wake. Its culture changed along with the size. The original organizational structure had three internal tiers, strict protocols, and skimpy resources, which were pledged but rarely paid by member states. It evolved into excessive funds, fewer formalities, and more camaraderie among diplomats. For example, the recently unified New Republic of Korea Mission occupied the entire thirty-eighth floor, which memorialized the famous thirty-eighth parallel of the ancient Korean War.

The membership was hosted by the Honorable Myung E. Kim, ambassador-at-large. She was to become a lightning rod of the international social set, noted for her beauty, talent as a former concert pianist, intellect, and popular parties. Gaining entry to her event-filled soirées was a prize sought by all, and her handpicked staff was noted to attend to every whim of all diplomats. Financing of her enterprise was pledged in each nation-state's annual dues and was always paid promptly. This was a century of progress in global diplomacy, as religious wars didn't exist. Ambassador Kim became a primary source for professional persuasion that sought a perfected art of encomiums to settle disputes among colleagues or nation-states. Her influence contributed to the future survival of mankind. The outcome of the debate on the proposed Moses Referendum would be decisive for her and everyone else.

The findings of Moses and his suggested referendum were lodged with the convening authority of the UN for disposition. After all, the future of civilization could well depend upon the results. In its essence, the Moses alternatives for mankind's survival turned on astronomy, oceanography, geology, and sociology. There wasn't any internationally recognized power or organization, other than the UN, that could manage this resulting conundrum. Of course, over its 169-year existence since 1945, the generational changes in its culture were palpable and paralleled the changing world and the consequences of reducing the stresses of religious wars on Earth and their geometric stress on the universe. These consequences of changing such strident behavior included more sanguine, but also created the crucial issue of progressively overpopulating the planet.

The worldwide military-industrial complex comported with the new prosperity of homogenized religion. They required national defense cartels to retool to meet new demands of promptly providing humane needs and improve living standards. Former weapon conglomerates used their accumulated financial muscle to reinvent themselves into infrastructure engineering companies to accommodate the explosive population growth seeded by longer lives, fewer wars, medical breakthroughs, and accelerated birth rates. These former military-industrial complexes had the resources, connections, and know-how to keep pace with new peacetime needs. Reallocating revenues heretofore earmarked for war to this new gluttonous hydra, which was a no-brainer for most international corporations and nation-state politicians because they maintained full employment.

Within a century, the military-industrial complex of the world morphed into Homeland Infrastructure Development Agencies (HIDA), a partnership between government and industry. Ambassador Kim oversaw HIDA, giving women of the world equality at the end of the first century of the third millennium, all because of homogenizing religion. Her objective was to ingratiate herself into HIDA, thereby influencing emigration, investigation, and contract negotiations. She was determined to launch a worldwide recognition movement to exchange religious holidays for unified Homeland Inspiration Days (HID holidays), thereby ingratiating herself socially with the populace to influence political elections and enshrine HIDA and its annual budget into the hearts and minds of the people. Ambassador Kim of the UN was celebrated throughout the world. Diplomacy had a new definition by the centennial.

Meanwhile, sequestered away in the Viennese annex of the UN was a GPO known as the Office for Outer Space Affairs. Staffed at first by outliers who combined scientific knowledge with mysticism to seek answers to the unanswerable, the office compiled a compendium of theories that gained traction as time went on. Then, at the centennial, these theories were paraded out for further scrutiny by the scientific community. They included studies on Paraspermya, thoughts on how microorganisms from outer space cause earthborn diseases, or UFOlogy, and perceptions of the UFOs. Also, noosphere was studied, noting the possibility of evolution leading humanity toward perfect unity. From the string theory, there arose the principle of holography wherein the universe was perceived as three-dimensional when it might have been only a two-dimensional hologram. The principle was supported by the anomaly of the global dream only a century before on the same day, at the same time of sleep, and in all the relevant languages of humanity. Any and all abstract theories were dusted off for further investigation by dream interpreters domiciled in every nation-state.

The Council on Longevity noted the rate of attrition in human life slowed considerably from 372 million deaths caused by religious wars and the addition of offspring of those saved for over two millennia. The council projected a net annual global population increase of 20 percent longer lives and greater fertility commencing in the third millennium to populate an ever-shrinking landmass caused by global warming, pollution, and rising seas. They also warned that the energy required to support a population explosion, including climate control, could generate as much stress on the cosmic environment as the violence and death perpetrated by religious wars. Potable water needs, however, appeared to be adequately resolved earlier by relocating glaciers. The Moses Commission was again retained to deal with spatial and other life-support systems conclusively.

After four generations of world peace, the UN was transformed from a premier international peacemaking organization into an ineffective yet imposing interloper into the most trivial disputes among nation-states until the advent of anomalous dreams. The UN bureaucracy grew to enormous proportions as working for it was deemed one of the cushiest jobs. Diplomats and staff members of every nation vied for assignment to it and, by extension, the orbit of Ambassador Kim.

The lack of intense concentration that the presiding secretary-general and members of the Security Council paid to the extensive report from the Moses Commission on saving humanity was evident by their insistence on reading no further than the executive summary appearing on the few front pages. In essence, the report presented four options to save humanity from the unforeseen consequences of homogenizing religion. They included a menu of rash solutions, each of which favored geology, astronomy, oceanography, or sociology. Time frames for implementing one or another ranged from ten to one hundred years or two hundred years to infinity. Project costs for each remedy were pegged at 100 billion US dollars, 1 trillion US dollars, 3 trillion US dollars, and higher. It concluded with a strong recommendation for a worldwide referendum to decide on which direction or combinations thereof the future of humanity would take.

The daunting prospect of deciding on an irrevocable course to preserve the earth for future generations was fraught with a collective fear of making a fatal mistake. The canopy of protected peace from religious wars was already a century old, and the unforeseen consequences were existential. Compounding it was not an option, so the mission of the UN was to thoroughly distill the available options and direct the consequent referendum toward the best chances for survival of humanity. To discern and rank them, a feasibility study of Moses's recommendations was to be undertaken before a referendum would be offered to the people of the world in whose hands the final decision resided.

Because every living person had an existential interest in the outcome, a search for an independent and qualified research consultant was not an option. Following a six-month search, the UN search committee unanimously recommended a completely vetted NGO active in international governing, societies, business, science, and the arts to opine on the feasibility on how to save mankind, subject to a final referendum by the very same body. The World Council on Futurity was chosen to investigate and opine on the Moses Commission's options to sustain humanity far into the future.

THE WORLD COUNCIL ON FUTURITY

The World Council on Futurity Inc. (WCF) was formed by the UN in Hamburg, Germany, early in the twenty-first century with a mission to independently review and comment to the UN on a myriad of nation-state proposals that served their constituents and future generations. With locations throughout the globe, each branch contained specialized experts in environment, measuring risks/rewards of global fiscal dilemmas, renewable energy technologies, nuclear physics, education and housing, and individual rights. The WCF claim to fame, however, was by the discovery of their chairman, J. Von Uexhule, of a calculus-based, logarithmic formulae of high dimension that could predict the outcome of the most trying dilemmas with uncanny certainty. The amplituhedron calculated unlimited interactions instantly at a time when sophisticated physics was unlikely to have the ability to conclude anything at all. Managing a range of input from the quantum state to big data volume was accomplished with mind-boggling speed and accuracy. They began in the year 2114 to determine feasible options to save humanity and the planet.

THE FEASIBILITY STUDY

Bound to not interfere with the free will humans exercised toward their ultimate destiny, Aliennus, using the accumulated knowledge of Paraspermya, took note of the unforeseen but highly probable relapse that might occur after the feasibility study ended. The gigantic programs under consideration were reversed interments, recontouring mountains, land reclamation, martian emigration, and harnessing fulminology.

Regarding harnessing fulminology, it was imagined from the collective human knowledge stored in Paraspermya that, regardless of atmospheric density, lightning is a likely phenomenon of planets, such as Venus, Jupiter, and Saturn, and is present at any other celestial body possessing an atmosphere. It is always manifested by supercharged bolts. Earth launched the satellites Pioneer and Cassini-Huygens to confirm this phenomenon. Harnessing and storing their electrical energy for interstellar travel would be far more efficient than any known fuel-based or solar propulsion by 500×4 from a ubiquitous source at an average of 4 billion bolts per storm from any suitable atmosphere.

An orbiting space station tows an electrical storage device to capture a high energy plasma channel that averages three miles in length on Earth and can be equipped to instantaneously retransmit them anywhere for any purpose. More research is required for other planets. The technology for harnessing five hundred mega joules of energy from a single bolt and redistributing it to a controlled environment, while still a work in process, is the long-term permanent solution to energize mankind while traveling or domiciled. Unlimited electrical energy, once harnessed, can drive any environmental need.

When, how, and to whom to convey radical ideas that arose for survival, was the challenge of the twenty-second century, subject to an individual study of each one, and a remedial solution, if any.

Generations of people learned about the original dream from depictions in books and from word of mouth as handed down through the generations. One aspect everyone agreed with was it was dreamt at the exact same time while in deep REM in every language, in everybody's sleep cycle. The phenomenon was since repeated but limited to subset specialists to add to their considerable expertise. Up until this occurrence, only one like dream was experienced, and that was worldwide and one hundred years ago. The message of a third universal dream explained the emerging changes.

CODIFYING HUMAN RIGHTS FOREVER

When practicing religionists left their home country, their beliefs and national constitution, if any, were left behind, and all adhered to the religious practices, civil, and criminal laws of the host country. Passports or visas didn't entitle foreigners to practice their religion if it was anathema to the host country. Fear of proselytizing turned into a legal infraction with consequences. These conditions became widely known among the 4,200 worldwide religions to the extent it was assumed violators expected retribution. Religious rights only went so far. Retribution took different forms: If Africana Tswana rituals were violated, the offender was ostracized without appeal and restitution was swift and costly to the offender. Sentencing under Waqf Islamic Koranic law consisted of physical punishment, depending upon the social status of the offender. Extracting physical vengeance for these victimless crimes ranged from victimless crimes (Hadd) included blood-letting for the infidel (Quisas), with pecuniary damages if in a business disputes (Diya), and just wrist slapping for elitists (Tazir). A century ago, your ancestors dreamt of ridding the world of religious intolerance, which was causing violence, murder, and stress. What they didn't know was the accumulation over two millennia caused great discomfort among the dark matter that bound the universe that posed an existential threat to planet Earth. Their commitment to homogenizing religion restored confidence that this abomination would end and restore equilibrium in the distribution of stress, or gravity, among the cosmos.

To assure the permanence of this solution, your generation can begin the task of memorializing your commitment to homogenizing religion, which you have tried and succeeded to incorporate into your daily lives for four generations. Now, in the third millennium, you must begin the task of crafting a manifesto, charter, and a bible to ensure homogenizing religion will last until eternity, knowing that every molecule and every atom in the universe, whether living or innate, must function in their natural state of stress arising from an unknown beginning to an unimaginable end. That truth alone obligates humanity to never again encroach on that order.

A FEASIBILITY REPORT ON LONG-TERM HUMAN SURVIVAL

WORLD FUTURE COUNCIL INC. HAMBURG, GERMANY

A COMPENDIUM OF THE REPORT ON LONG-TERM HUMAN SURVIVAL

FOR THE SECRETARY-GENERAL OF THE UNITED NATIONS

COMMENCEMENT: AD 2114
COMPLETION: AD 2139

The Feasibility Report

(unabridged)

Contents

THE FEASIBILITY REPORT ABSTRACT

PREAMBLE

This abstract was developed in accordance with the mandate of the year 2014 by the secretary-general of the United Nations to opine on predetermined recommendations for the survival of humanity. We worked for twenty-five consecutive years and engaged 1,500,000 employees to identify, locate, confirm, and accumulate 99.9 percent of the relevant knowledge available. We have analyzed and validated primary and secondary sources, then sorted and cross-checked them to ensure their veracity. Only then did we accept their submission as definitive. We adopted best practices in a secure environment, sought public opinions, and outlier recommendations subject to authentication and confirmation of their relevance and factual perceptions.

METHODOLOGY

The methodology adopted for this enormous project required dispatching thousands of vetted specialists in every scientific discipline to each continent that provided a seamless rate for attrition. They searched and retrieved only factual data concerning geology, oceanography, engineering, architecture, aerospace, physics, astral physics, sociology, psychology, medicine, and other specialties and subspecialties for purposes of collecting, translating, verifying, then digitizing those vetted data for further study and codification to any of the five proposals.

Each silo of relevant facts was cataloged and stored into the latest generation of the Watson Big Data platform, which has infinite capacity to evaluate and integrate the totality of the world's knowledge into its artificial intelligence (AI) predictive algorithm architecture to track and resolve conflicts, resulting in the purest collection of world knowledge ever assembled to solve a big existential problem. This methodology results in a factual absorption rate of all known world data of 99.9 percent.

BACKGROUND

THE PROPOSAL

Without radical changes in life-support systems, the future of humanity as we now know it is not sustainable beyond the third millennium as a direct consequence of homogenized religion and scientific and medical breakthroughs to a lesser but important extent. Absent religious wars and their accelerating deaths, human population is projected to grow at a net rate of 20 percent per decade during the second and third millennia until reaching the equivalent of 20.5 billion inhabitants.

The remedies offered by the Moses Commission, after their lengthy and exacting study to assure human existence in perpetuity as well as the planet Earth as independent cosmic life forces (ICLF), can be defined as a three-phase plan consisting of two interim phases and permanent fixes:

Short-term measures are over a period of twenty years to permanently alter existing land use to reclaim up to 10 percent of existing landmass for a total of 3 million square miles devoted to people who used to occupy the planet for present and future habitation, at a cost of 20 trillion US dollars.

Mid-term measures include two land projects of recontouring uninhabitable landmass. It will be done in two stages over a period of one hundred and two hundred years, providing additional 18 million square miles of habitable space and preventing erosion of another 13 million square miles, at a total cost of 230 trillion US dollars, in tranches of 100 trillion US dollars over the first hundred year and an additional 130 trillion US dollars over the next hundred year.

Long-term measures include irreversible emigration from planet Earth to Mars, which is essential within the next 500 years, for despite best efforts, planet Earth can't ever support a human population of 20.5-plus billion without exterminating almost every other species of animal and vegetation. That, too, will end humanity. The cost to harness fulminology and develop travel technology is infinite. In addition, life support systems must be developed to survive a winter surface temperature of $-55^{0}C$ and a summer temperature of $+20^{0}C$. The landmass is also covered by a sand depth of 400 kg, which needs to be managed, and protection from surface storms of 400 km per hour will be necessary.

CONSEQUENCES AND SOLUTIONS

The case for homogenizing religion was made long ago to everyone's satisfaction, then implemented and proven over a century to benefit humanity and the universe from the extraordinary stress caused by religious wars. However, unintended consequences arose of a magnitude as threatening to human existence, as was the cause it intended to cure and the medicine turned out to be as toxic as the disease.

The Moses Commission, after a considerable effort over many years, adopted several proposals—none of which were contemplated before—to remedy the unintended consequences of homogenizing religion. We are to determine the feasibility of these allegoric solutions and share them with the United Nations along with other relevant observations. Our findings are briefly discussed below in this abstraction of the report.

1. The workload required for several proposals is beyond human capacity to achieve.

The proposals made by the commission require the physical labor of 1 billion workers for twenty-four hours, seven days a week over a period of two to twenty contiguous generations. This impossible feat is the very antithesis of a quality-of-life existence, rendering any need for human life problematical. Notwithstanding the outstanding advances made in engineering and mechanical, electrical, and technological power and that yet to be discovered fulfillment of the commission's proposals are beyond today's demolition and reconstruction capabilities with one notable exception. The nature of these untenable consequences of homogenizing religion forces us, as finders of fact, to think in radical ways. The future of humanity is in a molten state, and we are charged to solidify it into an unimpeachably sound and foolproof discipline and stabilize all notions that oriented the world for millennia and are now wobbling. Educated beliefs about reality can turn out to be in error or, worse, lies. Nothing less than an existential threat can produce a comparable effect. Even the discovery of alien life wouldn't so decompose the accumulated knowledge of the world. What then is the exception?

2. When the exception becomes the rule, all else is simply filler.

An indisputable fact is that stress throughout the universe results from the physical arrangement between living and innate matter. All else is subjective, and that alone affects how mind and matter interfaces in defiance of common sense. All else that exists is not what it seems other than something one-dimensional under constant stress. That is the dominant reason for codifying and collating all knowledge in the latest iteration of Watson, for the first time in human history, while reserving 0.1 percent as a doomsday switch.

3. **The availability of a pool of complete knowledge in one place was the ultimate exception that would transform humanity for all time with precise predictability.**

However dispositive the forthcoming solutions might be, they are not totally immune to consequences between a known beginning and predictable end. Risk—a human condition however mitigated—still exists.

4. **The sheer volume of physical labor required to reshape Earth to accommodate a geometrical increase in human population is both quantitatively and qualitatively beyond the scope of humanity.**

Projected work schedules leave little time for basic social needs other than sleeping and eating. The very effort to preserve humanity under such extreme circumstances is problematical. However, the case for universal knowledge and prophetic insight to complete the project in the short and long term is available and creditable to Watson. However, the confidence to remake the planet based solely on these phenomena is a nonstarter. Provisions must be made to ensure the quality of human life in perpetuity if it is to succeed in saving the species. Opportunities for continuity of education, leisure, and psychological and emotional needs must be intergenerational to adapt to radical changing environments. These imports have a direct effect on the quality of human life for future generations.

5. The solution requires immediate marshalling of the world's resources.

The resources needed include political, physical, scientific, economic, and technological expertise to invent and develop, then fabricate and deploy, a worldwide robotic network, populated with exhaustive artificial intelligence provided and controlled by Watson to ensure perfect precision in performing assigned tasks.

This self-teaching and replicating robotic architecture provides a continuity of physical labor with specificity and conformity to plans beyond any human capability by a factor of 1,0002. Using error-free robotic work tribes safeguard the quality of life for humanity while progressing toward race survival. The subworld of augmented reality enveloped linear algebra of vector spaces and matrix decomposition; the calculus of partial derivatives and function gradients, e.g., computer programming in the Python 5.7 or C++ language resulted in a robotic network immune to insects, diseases, injuries, or food breaks. Robot swarms, while heterogeneous, must be terrain perceptive, functioning in celestial, terrestrial, or submersible atmospheres, fully automated and agile efficient to demolish, excavate, and reconstruct planet-altering projects, thus ensuring humanity a good quality of life while existential solutions progress. Focusing the world scientific and industrial complex on fabricating AI robotics, defined as computer literate software, to function as close as possible to human cognition—including visual perception, speech recognition, data, and predictive decision-making capabilities—deserves the highest priority as soon as possible.

AI robotic technology coupled with the mastery of Watson is crucial to the salvation of humanity. Future iterations of Watson will be taught to read the world's knowledge stored within it and process our words as subjects, not objects of human consciousness—including history, art forms, literature, philosophy, mathematics, poetry, and even ancient mythology, and then function as a master of toil for planet-size projects. The real challenge today for our survival tomorrow isn't whether we should make machines that can think but rather if we should. Our future, as seen today, is sordid in two respects: those being unintended consequences of homogenizing religion and those burying civilization in an avalanche of permanent physical labor that can leave humanity with nothing to distinguish it from innate material resources. By amplifying AI robotics, we can reconfigure terrestrial resources into structures that maximize their needed utility faster than humans do by ten thousand to one.

SOCIOECONOMIC UPHEAVALS

Gigantism of the solutions under consideration necessitates an economic regimen of disambiguation (EROD) that meets every routine instantly, couched in a confidential, secure, and trustworthy architecture. Watson designed Clio dynamics, a new economic system of digital platforms employing cryptocurrency and blockchain exchanges to meet humanity's needs. Each transaction is monitored and administered through a universal market-exchange, the Eigen Trust, which was limited to 900 million accounts a hundred years ago. But now, thanks to Watson, it is capable of processing 500 million transactions per second. Also, as a minor appendage to Watson's latest iteration, it is capable of storing unalterable records of each individual and real-time transaction by instant replication, thereby recording transfer of ownership imminently to ensure permanence to worldwide economics.

As new industries emerge, some using 3D printing to fabricate usable products of any type of material, we can reduce the work in process to nanoseconds. Specialties like engineering and architecture were commoditized by using interactive, off-the-shelf flash drives. Advanced medical diagnostics were available by plug-in methodologies that measure and alter human genealogy, physicality, chemistry, and emotions to maintain optimal individual health throughout a lifetime. Newly discovered techniques of fulminology, a harnessing of clean lightning energy, was employed ubiquitously to meet all pollution-free energy needs of society at large. Every process and person was tied to one or another of Watson's ever-expanding artificial intelligence platforms that stored and acted on unlimited data that was subjected to a continuous stream of updating.

The growing population on Earth showed no relief. Competition between individuals for fame and fortune, once a tradition, became an extinct concept to be replaced by innovations to maintain a qualitative life on an overcrowded planet. Clio dynamics provided each living person with an annual stipend equal to their individual needs as determined by Watson, who recorded each transaction of income, investment, and expense and their individual quality based on social needs for each person. Individual wealth accumulation of cryptocurrency is gained by profiting in the usual way, from ownership or investing or trading, after meeting all society's personal and standard-of-life needs, given the gravity of the survival plans as weighted and recommended by Watson. Clio dynamics was specifically designed to assure each individual that life was worth living in conjunction with the gigantic undertaking to remedy the existential consequences of homogenizing religion. The crowding out of old cultural mores resulting from homogenizing religion provided both a century of peace and consequent projection of unsustainable populating. The portents of past reverence, wars, and deaths became memorable whispers, replaced by a universal commitment to the survival of humans, one hundred years afterward.

A DREAM CODA FOR THE FEASIBILITY REPORT

While engaged in preparing to publish our conclusions and recommendations, the editorial staff of the World Future Council experienced a common dream on the same day at the same time and place. Similar phenomena were known to occur from time to time during the early twenty-first century. What was striking to all, however, was the clarity and alacrity of its content.

Land and sea burials are dead. Yes, the pun was intended, but the seriousness remains. They must stop, as they are unsustainable because there is not enough land and too many people. The amount of planet Earth devoted to graveyards is monotonically increasing and threatening to completely consume Earth's surface. For example, the inhabitable surface land area of Earth is 37 billion acres, and the death rate averages eight per one thousand people per day. As the population exploded due to homogenized religion, Earth will soon become one big graveyard.

Bio solutions are the answer. Interments by digging graves or erecting mausoleums or polluting cremation by fire must give way to liquefaction by alkaline hydrolysis since 66 percent of human bodies are water and 20 percent is protein, both of which are conducive to alkaline dissolution—a carbon footprint of one-third of which is caused by traditional cemetery usage. Albeit a short-term solution to the consequences of homogenizing religion, purging such aesthetic anthropomorphisms that never remotely imitated life but defied nature instead could have a far-reaching effect on the planet and all humanity. This is only a beginning.

CONCLUSION OF THE
MOSES COMMISSION

We agree and highly recommend, subject to the certain provisos, those short-term, medium-term, and long-term solutions developed by the Moses Commission, described in detail in the complete feasibility report, and incorporated above by reference in this abstract, subject to the following provisory:

Proviso

It is imperative that a decade be dedicated to a preparation platform that will serve as the foundation for the entire program prior to commencing the first phase of the survival plan. The preparations should include the following:

1. Design and code essential AI architectures for iterative Watson control functions needed to manage robotic labor phases for each project, and instantly operate a new worldwide economic system. This is easily a ten-year project.

2. Start up new industries utilizing a 3D-print process to engineer and fabricate a generation of self-replicating AI robotics to perform twenty-four hours a day, seven days a week, and at a physical workload equal to one hundred times more than is expected from traditional laborers. AI robotics are currently beating humans in a growing number of narrow tasks they are designed for; however, the specialty field is not focused on AI general intelligence, but deep learning platforms producing breathtaking results in particular areas like laborious tasks. Electronic commands, when coupled with voice instructions, determine the syntactic structure of copious labor tasks. With a decade of

progress, AI robotics will be controlled by a Watson iteration to replicate human labor tasks with minimal human oversight.

3. Harness fulminology as an evergreen power source for use in all environments.

4. Reconfigure existing social systems to assure at least two distinct cultures: one for a liberalized quality of life and another for the scientific control of newly formed AI robotic tribes that ensure a continuous work force for generations of humanity to prepare for survival of the species.

5. Legal systems of nation-states must be revamped so as to be available to anyone who needs access to decent, just, and practical laws absent of suppression in the ancient names of unjust, dirty, or unenforceable. The laws, as they stand now, are a gratuitous insult to modern society, most of which do not consider most prohibitions indecent. The function of law is to protect people's rights and not those of a small minority, previously known as religious influence. Laws are now needed to distinguish between prohibiting acts without information and acquiescence regarding their concepts available to the public. We suggest a country-by-country referendum on existing laws explained in plain text, along with proposals for revisions for whenever people unite in their demands; freedom rather than suppression wins.

THE ONLY SOLUTION FROM MOSES COMMISSION

By the irrevocable referendum, the Moses Commission recommends the adoption of a final plan of survival. We disagree. The preponderance of evidence irrefutably leads to the conclusion that herculean efforts must be undertaken if humans are to survive the consequences of homogenizing religion, which began a hundred years ago. The nature of the remedies recommended to escape omnicide is of such complexity as to confuse the public at large in an open discourse. Scientists, industrialists, economists, and other experts are eminently qualified to understand the cause and effect of the remedies proposed in this extensive report. Politicians, pollsters, public speakers, and marketers are the least qualified, often engaged in false prophesies, creating confusing opinions and mass hypnosis. They are best left to count the votes. The WCF prefers the feasibility report be debated and voted upon by a body of elected representatives of each nation-state in the UN, and a final decision, that by its nature is irreversible, to commit future generations to specific plans for survival.

Reversing Interments

This project was estimated to take up to twenty years and cost 20 trillion US dollars to reclaim 3 million square miles of habitable land used exclusively for interments. Watson contains verified records of 475,213 cemeteries in 238 countries and predictive AI methodology reveals 1.9 million worldwide containing 5 billion human remains. Disinterring and hydrolyzing all contents and new deaths results in land reclamation of 3.25 million square miles at a total cost of 17 trillion US dollars over a contiguous seventeen-year project, including the development of the hydrolysis industry.

Worldwide, this short-term measure includes an unbreakable continuity of employing 25 million people for a twenty-four-hour-a-day, seven-day workload over the project period. New platforms of robotic architecture already conceived, tested, programmed, and replicated for use on selected areas of this short-term project. These robotic swarms will respond to Watson as a central control and to cues from their environment and one another. Until the project is robotically populated, a human workforce must be impressed for research, development, design and fabricating, programming, and management to meet the land reclamation goals of the plan during the early years. The projected telescoping of the original time frame and cost will be realized when the robotic labor force reaches 205,000 over the remaining life of the project. Details are contained in the full report.

Recontouring Mountains and Land Reclamation

This medium-term phase is expected to last for one to two hundred years at a cumulative cost of 230 trillion US dollars to employ 60 million persons and reclaim 18 million square miles of land to expand Earth's habitable landmass by 60 percent, the absolute terrestrial limit. Perfecting six hundred thousand Watson-controlled AI robots over the project life accelerates completion by 50 years to 150 years (25 percent less) and reduces real project costs from 230 trillion US dollars to 195 trillion (15 percent less). This doesn't include the substantive savings from eliminating cost overruns by substituting human labor with AI robotic production efficiencies. A failure to spend on overruns could exceed the entire project cost. Details are described in the full report.

Interplanetary Emigration

The synchronic goal to which the above existential phases are devoted can be realized within five hundred years. It includes a mass emigration to the planet Mars with a landmass equivalent to Earth (29 million sq. miles), despite the planet's smaller size (1/2 the diameter of Earth). The challenge for humanity is to render it habitable. Costs and details of this final phase of humanity's survival plan are enumerated in the full report.

Assumptions

Common to all above phases are the following: impressing Watson and its iterative in a continuous stream of present-day knowledge for use across all phases of the survival plan; harnessing fulminology; perfection of self-replicating, artificially intelligent management, and laconic robotics; and the distinct separation of this millennium-sized plan for the survival of humanity and every-day needs of human civilization. Watson-controlled AI, self-replicating robotics for management and physical labor, is crucial to maintaining the human spirit for the twenty generations that evolved from an ever-increasing population. Details are discussed above and in the full report.

Opinion of the World Council on Futurity

This is the largest project ever undertaken in the history of mankind and is existential for humanity. The elaborate methodology is required for planning, preparation, and execution throughout the third millennium. During this multigenerational commitment, an irrevocable treaty for of human survival (TFHS) among nation-states of Earth is indispensable to success.

No such agreement was necessary for homogenizing religion. Such a treaty correlates abstract ideas and principles, not causes, and discerns complexities and timelines of the global plan to its unimaginable end.

TREATY FOR HUMAN SURVIVAL

HONORING the unanimous agreement among Earth's nation-states to reconfigure its landmass to accommodate a burgeoning human population emanating from the advent of homogenizing religion a century ago and further recognizing its existential nature began with the signing of this treaty in AD 2114, for and continuing for a period of not less than five hundred (500) years;

ACCEPTING that interplanetary emigration is essential to the survival of the human species;

DETERMINING any effort, cost, expense, new product, or robotic developments, and all existing and new knowledge gained and retained by Watson or its iterative, are equal in ownership by all mankind;

ASPIRING to prevent international conflicts during the course of this multigenerational endeavor; and

RELYING on past treaties and principles governing the activities of nation-states in common purpose agreements, as in the law of the sea (admiralty law); exploration and use of outer space; the rescue and return of astronauts; the convention of the international liability for damage caused by space objects; the convention on registration of objects launched into outer space, etc.

All Who Sign This Document Have Agreed to the Following:

All provisions of this treaty relating to the opening of the earth shall also apply to all other celestial bodies within our solar system except insofar as extant legal norms remain in force or if extraterrestrial matter reaches Earth by natural means.

All exploration and use of activities contemplated under this treaty on Earth and in outer space shall conform to the international law and to the charter of the United Nations.

All reclaimed and habitable land shall be used by all nation-states, exclusively for peaceful and humane purposes.

All hostile acts or threats thereof among nation-states are prohibited on Earth and in outer space.

Nuclear devices of any description are permanently banned on Earth or in orbit around any celestial body unless specifically prescribed in the plan as amended.

Opening of the earth for purposes of reclaiming habitable landmass, the methodology employed, access to Watson, and outer-space exploits shall be the province of all mankind, carried out pari passu for the benefit and in the interests of each nation-state, guided by principles of cooperation and mutual assistance to all in this existential undertaking.

Reclaimed habitable land on Earth and in outer space is not subject to sovereign appropriation by any claim of nationalization, use or occupancy, or any other means. All humanity claims a right to exploration and occupancy when certified, without discrimination on the basis of equality in accordance with the international law and the provisions of this treaty.

TWG opines the only available chance for human survival rests in the plan, depicting reversing interments, recontouring mountains and ocean land reclamation, and eventual interplanetary emigration. The details of which are contained in the complete report on the prospects for human survival, which began on 2114 and was completed on AD 2139, containing five hundred thousand pages, referenced in this abstract, and to which we refer you.

THE MOTHER OF
ALL DEBATES

THE FIRST TIME HUMANS AND NOT NATURE DECIDED THE FATE OF A PLANET

Perceived encounters formed the basis for every anomaly experienced on Earth during the first and second millennium. Ancient hypotheses were founded in patterns of art, engineering, and in periods of greater cognition, prophesies, cave drawings, pyramids of Egypt, Stonehenge, the theory of relativity, WWI and II, and nuclear tests. Numerous motives were imagined for human abduction, including purposes of genital examinations, altering the human genome, survival of an alien race, and destruction of Earth; yet no scientific evidence was ever discovered to justify these hysterics, eyewitness accounts notwithstanding.

Proving the axiom that little knowledge is a dangerous thing, the theory of quantum entanglement, also known as the entropy of entanglement, arose during the second millennium. It posited the universe as two-dimensional although it was seen as three-dimensional, much like a hologram. This mind-twisting notion proposed that gravity evident in the space-time quadrant comports with quantum fields as small as an atom designed by aliens to deliberately distort our view of the cosmos. This was soon followed by the blue skies theory, a theory researched without a clear goal that entertained proposals to radically change the way people thought about anything and everything. Then there were those whose mindset changed when facts conflicted with their beliefs, and they acted upon what they concluded was righteous. They were motivated by piety and reverence, for the most part, to the exclusion of scientifically proven facts. In these cases, their cognition was altered by how they thought the world should function, as though sacred values in the supernatural are immune to facts of life. Magnificently constructed temples were often thought of as portals to heaven though built by mankind for meditating. These were not dumb people who strained reasoning to enhance morality rather than face facts.

Others pursued a passion for mysticism to corral the universe down to a singular belief. Almost everything inexplicable became a gateway to universal panocracy. The sea of anomalies flowed like waves of electromagnetic energy, and the planet glowed with as many extraterrestrial thoughts as light, radio, and microwaves. It was as though the earth itself was thinking.

One such theory came from a Jesuit priest, trained as a scientist and a religious mystic. Oxymorons like this were not rare. This priest viewed the world as evolving from a dead planet to one of mindless biological life, ever certain vegetation would lead to a universal consciousness that was housed in a thinking sphere circling above the biosphere, accessible to evolving matter. He called this a knowledge sphere. The closest that people came to realizing this in the second millennium was when they traded mindless network TV in exchange for absorbing scientific information over the internet. Of course, it soon changed into another mindless social forum.

A host of turning points combined to become a tipping point in 2019 as the influence of homogenizing religion on humanity was more powerful than all scientific, social, legal, or military doctrines or phenomenon in any past years. It eventually liberated generations to live free from mind-bending superstitions and other imaginary fears. Ancient discoveries contributed in fragments, but none could match the unshackling of people as did homogenizing religion. The steam engine, electricity, internal combustion engines, aircrafts, computers, and the internet didn't answer the fundamental intrigues of life, the earth, and the universe as did homogenizing religion. When the big debate took place, the people had no idea about the nature of the matter, the cosmos, consciousness, time, intelligence, or the purpose of life. This radical rupture between reality and perception could be attributed to generations of wasted resources, fighting religious wars until a dream of human enlightenment caused a core change in human behavior.

THE DEBATE

The Forum: UN headquarters in New York City, United States

The Participants

Moderator:	The Secretary-General of the UN (Dr. Semmelweis)
Proponents:	Hon. Jose Adamo, President of South American Continent
	Hon. Hiro Akemi, President of Japan and Far Eastern Continent
	Hon. Yang Chen, President of China
	Hon. Kim Chee, President of Korea
	Hon. Barak Trudeau, President of North America
Antagonists:	Hon. Sven Klaus, President of Europe and Siberia
	Hon. Ben Johnson, President of Africa
	Hon. Vladimir Pushkin, President of Russia
Undecided:	Hon. Katherine Anna, President of Australia and surroundings
	Hon. Mathew Singh, President of India Hon. Ryan Dear, President of the Artic

DEBATE INTRODUCTION

The secretary-general, Dr. Semmelweis, began speaking, "At this first of many plenary sessions, we gather together to violate the laws of nature. Yes, you heard correctly. In other words, we are expected to create and perform miracles, which will determine the fate of our planet and survival of humans. The WCF completed the most comprehensive and factual study to ascertain how to survive the unintended consequences of homogenizing religion, undertaken and completed in the past one hundred years. That, too, was existential at the time. Now we are mandated to unanimously opine on the feasibility of surviving the consequences of that incomprehensible, but unavoidable, task after twenty-five years of relentless research, analysis, and fact-gathering contained in a five-hundred-thousand-page report, digitally available to all nation-state governments for further discussion.

"Until action plans are vetted, debated, and agreed to by the members, the feasibility report is classified as not available to the public to avoid confusion and prevent chaos from any misinterpretations of its earth-shattering recommendations, anyone of which can take up to twenty-five years to launch. All are multigenerational." He went on, "The emergence of artificial intelligence via adaptive computer programs is unlike the slow evolution of biological life and will race forward at the speed of light, and the apocalypse we seek to avoid requires a continuity of iterative, reproducing, and constantly adapting living code of knowledge to power Watson and the robots it drives. To that end, and to provide this assembly the benefits of expertise, I, as secretary-general of the United Nations, have vetted all experts proposed by nation-state members to debate each segment of the feasibility report in the assembly forum and arrive at a holistically acceptable outcome. The debaters will have five years to study the report and assemble their respective positions. The assembly is herewith adjourned until that time, sine die."

FIVE YEARS LATER

THE DEBATE COMMENCES

Dr. Semmelweis: Having had five years to examine all segments of the report, we have reconvened for the express purpose of discussing your observations. To begin, I call on the Honorable Jose Adamo, president of the South American continent.

President Adamo: While it is not possible to absorb so lengthy and crucial report of five hundred thousand pages in length within the allotted time, the South American member state group examined the abstract and several sections of the main body and found them to be comprehensible but possibly exaggerated. We are convinced, however, that absent radical action, the world as we know it cannot be reinvigorated sufficiently to host the future of humanity. Behavioral reform is a century-old endeavor to no avail, and so our desire for perpetuity by imitating nature by the cycle of rebirth becomes our Achilles heel. We agree with the theme of the report that mankind must master better reasoning than merely mimicking nature if we are to survive. The feasibility report fulfills the need for futuristic thinking, planning, and societal changes rather than contaminate essential progress with worthless wisdom of past ages. The South American continent proclaims its support in principle for the plan.

All Participants: [Applause and scattered jeers]

Dr. Semmelweis: I call on the president of the African nation-state group, the Honorable Ben Johnson, to approach the podium.

President Johnson: The voluminous feasibility report and independent opinion rendered by the World Council on Futurity (WCF) appears immersed in a mix of fictional realism, and it is for this reason, we of the African Continent oppose the conclusions as submitted. The underlying premise—upon which future generations are preordained to commit their labor, knowledge, and treasure—appears to be based on a philosophy that everything in the universe must exist somewhere, a conscious perception of phenomenalism that, when combined with the theory of externalism codifies nunc pro tunc what is merely a theory that the time dimension is multilayered so as to accommodate various cosmic locations. We reject that premise as illusionary as well as the conclusion that planet Earth is headed toward a final stage caused by unintended consequences of homogenizing religion one hundred years ago.

Finally, and based solely upon our cursory review, we are unnerved by a perceived need to alter the human body by inserting RFID chips for mind and communication control, and biologically altering human genomes, IVF selection and genes so as to supervise and control AI and robotic augmentation of our bodies to be smarter, stronger, and more capable than we are today in the year 2139, as well as protect the species against unknown diseases of the future. These challenges are among the most formidable as the underlying premise of the existential plan, which we reject.

Dr. Semmelweis: Thank you, President Johnson. And to all members of the assembly, you have now studied and heard protagonist and antagonist views of the feasibility report after just a cursory five-year review period, and one that barely penetrates the effort of the world's most brilliant experts who labored twenty-four hours, seven days a week on it for twenty-five years to save the human race from extinction. The facts contained therein are unquestionable, although one can disagree with the conclusions of people. Using your electronic desk button, please indicate to the chair your attitude as of today. This is a straw vote and nonbinding. Thank you.

Official vote counter: The current vote is 33 percent aye and 67 percent nay.

Dr. Semmelweis: I call on the Honorable Mathew Singh, president of India.

President Singh: In a zero-sum game, there are losers and winners, but nothing more. We are working to survive the consequences of homogenizing religion adopted by our ancestors one hundred years ago. They were the game then, and we are today. A century ago, the first ever universal dream was judged as divine intervention, a clincher for adopting and adapting the world to homogenizing religion, or they believed they would face certain extinction. They won over 4,200 religions, and we, as a species, are here one hundred years later. Such parallel interests make cooperation desirable. However, if we insist on nothing less than a zero-sum approach to common problems, then agreement, understanding, and a search for solutions are pointless. We of India are undecided as to the singularity and finality of the solution opined on by the WCF but pledge to join in the debate of understanding despite a fierce fear of a futuristic world so different from the one we are living in now."

Dr. Semmelweis: Within a span of only ten years, the General Assembly heard three distinctly different views of the solutions proposed by the greatest array of experts ever assembled, all of whom were supported by the most complete array of knowledge available to mankind. This demonstrates, conclusively, the chief savior of civilization is homogenizing 4,200 religions of one hundred years ago that evolved into the most malevolent mind virus that ever affected the universe and freed our minds to coalesce into a supermind on Earth to cooperate and join the galactic community. The formulae we require to perpetuate life five hundred years in the future are vastly different from those needed to recreate life of five hundred years past, and we are on the road to achieving them.

We now adjourn the General Assembly until five years hence to allow each nation-state the time frames requested by them to continue their examination and discourse of the feasibility report, and orient new individuals to study and actively participate in the second forthcoming debate on survival of the human race. Each nation-state will ponder the feasibility report informally among themselves during the second five-year hiatus.

Gathering informally in the ambassador's lounge, Barak Trudeau, Yang Chen, Sven Klaus, and Katherine Anna bantered their innermost thoughts back and forth in a trustful and confidential manner.

Sven Klaus, the European and Siberian president, said, "At a most critical phase in all of mankind, I sense a conspiracy among some members of the UN with the elitist groups of the society they represent. Under the guise of providing faux counsel and purporting to help us commit future generations to the singularity of purpose to save the human race, they will harm our constituents by kicking the can down the road, then leaving it to them to resolve."

"I am worried about such a narrow approach to an everlasting and irrevocable plan of action to save all of humanity. I am using nongovernmental experts who hold appropriate security clearances to shore up my analytical staff, and are you suggesting by so doing, I am pondering the imponderable?" asked Katherine Anna, president of Australia.

President Anna continued, "Would you rather tackle this existential dilemma like the clever fiction writer Jonathan Swift in the eighteenth century of the second millennium? You might recall, and you can verify with Watson, in *Gulliver's Travels*, he pondered how to efficiently break eggs before consuming them by their larger and not traditionally smaller ends. The debate went on for centuries, cost thousands of lives along the way until it was resolved by referendum that allowed for their breaking at the most convenient end according to each breaker's taste."

China's Yang Chen piped into the conversation by pointedly addressing Katherine Anna, "Are you suggesting a worldwide referendum on the fate of humanity?"

To which Barak Trudeau added, "Or shall we, at the United Nations, be the final arbiter, not by convincing the public at large, but by waiting until a generation of likely opponents die off?"

The group laughed at the rancor, but seeds of a referendum were planted. "Our concern, along with saving humanity of course, is maintaining national sovereignty. Should not each nation-state be solely responsible for carrying out a plan of action on its own territory, to which it agreed to by treaty, or are all of you contemplating a worldwide collusion of efforts wherein all sense of self-governing is ended?" asked Vladimir Pushkin, president of Russia.

Ryan Dear, president of the Arctic, laughingly replied, "Vladimir, are you contemplating a home delivery business venture for harnessing glaciers to fill the canyons of lower nation-states with potable water while the world burns? An all-Russian ice company!"

Robust laughter followed. Everybody laughed except for Pushkin.

AN ATTEMPT AT INSURRECTION

Simmering agitation by some members against adopting the feasibility report was caused by imaginary biases, suspect authors, distrust of Moses, and the WCF blanket endorsement of the findings. From time to time, during the ten-year oversight period, it appeared that prejudice and avarice were more important than the survival of the human race. High-octane emotions fueled resentment against the limited option of either acceptance or extermination. Women representatives were agitated and openly vowed that procreation was over if their offspring were subject to generations of hard labor without any assurances of the outcome. The more compliant representatives tried to reassure their female colleagues that the cultures of society at large would be exculpated from tasking but not managing the plan after it was adopted. In fact, the feasibility plan provided such protections. Notwithstanding all the safety factors to assure separate societies stay engaged as the feasibility plan progressed throughout the ages, a threat of sedition from the plan was newsworthy and spread among the various UN house organs.

THE DELEGATE'S DREAM

All 180 nation-state heads, along with their delegations of thousands, adjourned the second plenary session of the UN, which was held ten years after receiving the feasibility report and World Council opinion and, unknown to them, fifteen years before approving both following the Mother of All Debates. Their collective approval to irrevocably commit all future generations to a defined course to save mankind from obliteration once again. However, their struggle was not to be without transcendental guidance. Night approached, and the entire UN contingent slept and dreamt.

On March 11, 2014, your ancestors became unified in their understanding of the underlying law of the universe they occupied, and how complete compliance can assure survival of the human species. Today, one hundred years later, you will exercise your free will to do the same. Way back then, only a handful of folks understood such complexities, such as the theory of relativity, yet today every child knows it. The knowledge explosion, technological advances, and artificial intelligence provided by Watson made it possible to harness the whole of human knowledge since the beginning of time to assure the survival of humanity. Now the time has come for adding transcendental knowledge to answer such dilemmas as the big bang theory. But first, the distillation of universal knowledge is limited to that contained in the feasibility report, whose evidence, combined with generational updates, is the best bet for survival once implemented by you with generation-to-generation continuity. Once awake, this new revelation culled

*from your dream will save you and your descendants
as it once did for your ancestors".*

The next morning, Vladimir Pushkin summoned his staff of hundreds to the secure conference room at the Russia Embassy. Guards were posted to assure maximum privacy as he addressed the group. He arrived in a panic with an unshaven face and was still in his pajamas, robe, and sleeping cap, which happen to all be in the same colors as the Russian flag. He announced anxiously, "This meeting is *top secret*. Last night, I experienced a revelation in a dream, the details of which I vividly recall today. Our national policy of relative isolation, conspiring, creating turmoil, and actuating whenever possible must end *now*, and I mean that plurally and pedantically!

"There is no great difference between us and them. Through the employment of our propaganda, we can raise their views to our higher level and grapple together with the difficulties we are facing for generations to come. To begin with, we shall support the feasibility report, its solutions, and work together with all other nation-states to implement them."

Together, the invited audience's heads nodded in agreement and a slowly rising crescendo of applause accompanied by shout out of "Mr. President, we had the same dream!" was heard.

When the surprise and excitement died down, Pushkin continued, "We have all heard stories of the ancients experiencing the same dreams at the same time, to which they credit a change in world order to survive an existential threat or suffer the consequences of not doing anything about it. Today, we have firsthand experience with a similarly mysterious dream, but times are very different. They were shocked, but not paralyzed, by the dreamlike revelation one hundred years ago. We have the technology and accumulated knowledge on how to plan and execute the needed changes, and to attribute the immense undertaking before us to a dream is an insult to humanity. Also, no proof exists that any dream was ever a convening force of social change. Our Russian cognition, along with myself, pledge to the world our cooperation to save humanity, but we will never discuss or credit a dream for it with anybody outside of this room *ever!*"

Simultaneously, but at a different venue, Hon. Mathew Singh, president of India, summoned his UN staff to gather and discuss his epiphany. Imagine the surprise when he learned that every member also experienced the same dream at the same time as he. He wondered if they all came to the same conclusion. Rather than probe for an answer, Singh quickly regrouped and altered what otherwise would have been an explosive presentation into a strategic discussion on the need for a unified endorsement of the feasibility report. Rather than remaining undecided, as previously reported, he said, "When uncertainty, an all too human condition, was the best outcome from long deliberations, our ancestors always sought spiritual guidance to enhance their cognition. As far back as 5,000 BC, the sacred and massive texts of the Mahabharata and Rig Veda served that purpose, as they were thought to have evolved from mysterious superpowers.

"Fast-forward to today and when faced with the same uncertainty, we will persevere until we uncover and are convinced otherwise by the certainty of facts that ground us in reality. However, on occasion, the assemblage of facts requires a reshuffling of intrinsic knowledge to sharpen our views in fateful way, as what happened to us last night as we dreamt. Occasionally, sometimes only once in a lifetime, we experience an event not triggered by any assemblage of facts but nonetheless changes our views, perhaps by sharpening up an intrinsic knowledge or reassembling it in a faithful way as in last night. At times like this, it seems like the vastness of unknown knowledge is supreme when compared to that heretofore assembled by humanity. The unanimity of our accord to support the feasibility report and use the remaining fifteen years working to plan and implement it vis-à-vis our unfounded trepidations and doubts speaks to the breadth of our understanding. How we arrive at that decision should be a bond among us and one which we don't seek laurels for as a nation-state. We will provide a rationale for proceeding and hide how an inexplicable dream was the essence of it. After all, we live in an era of precise science."

The delegates of India all agreed.

All others at the UN representing governing nation-states and continents were equally privy to the universal dream and its hypnotic effect on how they perceived the proposed solution of the feasibility report. Despite the sudden unanimity of views among them, they had good cause to suspect it permeated the entire General Assembly, although nobody admitted to it. After all, how could the power of a contained dream be explained as the sole basis for endorsing a multigenerational project to change the planet? Best to keep it secret and convince the public that the unanimous decision by the UN to accept the report was arrived at following a multiyear and copious examination of the feasibility report and give value to the World Council's revered opinion.

Each voting delegation anxiously awaited the next meeting of the UN General Assembly.

THE UNITED NATIONS
RECONVENES

THE VOTE

Dr. Semmelweis: I hereby reconvene the General Assembly explicitly to vote on propositions. You have ten minutes to electronically vote aye or nay to the following three items: First, express your support or opposition to adopting the feasibility report after ten years of review by the members. Next, please vote on whether to release the unredacted report with our decision to the public at large. Third, you will vote on whether or not you agree to establish a date certain to execute an approved plan.

NoMonkeyBusines Poll Results		
	Vote Percent	
Proposition 1: Do you agree to adopt the feasibility report after ten years of review by the members?	Yes No	100% 0%
Proposition 2: Do you agree to release the unredacted report with our decision to the public at large?	Yes No	66% 34%
Proposition 3: Do you agree to establish a date certain to execute an approved plan?	Yes No	100% 0%

Dr. Semmelweis [continued]: The objections to proposition 2 are because some of you fear public confusion and chaos when they are faced with the omnicide that will be caused by inaction and the gigantism of the only options available for mankind to survive. Any resulting demand for a worldwide referendum is frightening under such circumstances. Since time is of the essence, they should put their confidence in their elected officials and appointments to the UN by proxy. Besides making public a five-hundred-thousand-page document, even an abstract of it would be overwhelming and subjected to misinterpretations, any and all of which are time-consuming to resolve. All conditions to the contrary for moral purposes of full disclosure would likely be received as a hoax or science fiction at best. This contemporary crisis isn't a struggle between diverse cultures or ancient religious favoring, but nevertheless remains a dilemma of all civilization that has no rival, for it charts the future of our whole world. We have to wonder if everyone has a right to decide their fate or be deprived of it by deception. That is the paradox we are facing. We will convene again tomorrow for the express purpose of addressing proposition 2.

PROPOSITION 2

Dream

Despite access to 99.9 percent of all accumulated human knowledge, stored and constantly updated by Watson over the past one hundred years, and honoring the courage of your ancestors back then to save humanity by accepting the challenge of homogenizing religion, the tasks before you remain daunting. Such problematic undertakings, albeit few and far between, are not zero-sum decisions, for they require exchanging the life forces and energies of earthbound generations with matter and antimatter of the cosmos. Trade-offs are human thinking. But how far backward or forward must this extraction of wisdom go? That depends solely on the DNA of your species and not any rule of scientific determinism.

One day, if there is to be any more for humanity, the elusive Euclidean time equations needed to put the big bang theory to rest will be revealed to your descendants. But for now, when you are threatened once again with annihilation, you must marshal your forces of reality as never before to devise methodologies and accurate predictive outcomes generations in advance to avoid it. All are remarkable achievements but lacks the essential dynamic qualities of space and time that must pace and guide you as they did your ancestors when they were faced with extinction one hundred years ago.

These solutions lie in externalism, a new dimension encompassing all past events within the universe that are archived at the speed of light and stored in the cloud, where the past, present, and future are equal and now is to time as here is to space. In this extreme dimension, decisiveness is arrived at unconsciously by pseudo-free will, a distinctly human trait that is couched in presentism. Paraspermya is a microbic roamer among the dark matter of the cosmos, possessing all thoughts and emotions of all who ever lived on Earth.

Each nushima is forever inscribed on this oasis of humanity that soars continuously among the planets where the dark matter is abundant, depending on human souls of the deceased for energy. It exists and perpetually grows to exert a metaphysical influence on every living person, subject somewhat to their free-will filter as each see fit. Your ancestors bear witness to this extraordinary galactic suasion.

If executed as depicted, the feasibility report represents the best chance for humanity to survive the approaching apocalypse. Since every living soul is faced with these inevitable consequences, they are entitled to reasoned transparency without the confusion and chaos. Therefore, a redacted version of an abstract of the report must be available to the public for absorption but not for a referendum!

VOTING ON PROPOSITION 2

The members of General Assembly of the UN awoke to a new day with renewed confidence in the feasibility report as the last bastion for survival of the species and voted unanimously to accept it as a mandate for all future generation to uphold. The remaining fifteen years allotted for reviewing it was to be spent updating and planning how to implement it by the year AD 2139. During the interim period, it was agreed by all governments, with the force of the international law, that Earth will be governed by the principles of the manifesto of homogenized religions.

AMENDMENTS

AMENDMENTS TO THE MANIFESTO FOR HOMOGENIZING RELIGION

SECTION I: DOCTRINES AND REALITY

Homogenizing religion harmonizes spiritual doctrines with reality.

FIRST AMENDMENT

Watson is forthwith designated as the primary archive of social experience and source of facts for changes.

SECTION II: HUMAN SUFFERING

Homogenizing religion is not indifferent to human suffering.

FIRST AMENDMENT

Homogenizing religion removes an important causation of stress-induced violence by human desperation. No longer burdened by compounding suffering by religionists, humanity can better attend to socio-generational harmony to meet, guide, and overcome existential threats.

SECTION III: DESPOTS

Homogenizing religion is of no use to despots.

First Amendment

With the advent of artificial intelligence, all worldly specialties become geometrically improved. Human decisions are fewer, the need for single-person governance is more of a caretaker function for an entire region, and individual aggrandizement is on the wane. Therefore, by virtue of this amendment, the need for civil governance is expanded to include facts as stated by Watson for others to consider while deliberating, and once agreed to, it irrevocably commits future generations to it. Future amendments, if any, follow the same process.

SECTION IV: BETWEEN CONSCIOUSNESS AND METAPHYSICALITY

Homogenizing religion respects the dichotomy between human consciousness and the metaphysical.

FIRST AMENDMENT

The advent of artificial intelligence in the form of Watson and its iterations enlarge the limited human capacity to think. Likely advances yet to be realized remove mysteries of humanity, and thereby empowers all future generations to covet other AI enhancements to ensure perpetuation of the species.

SECTION V: RIGHTS, PROPERTY, COMMERCE, AND SOCIETY

FIRST AMENDMENT

Facing palpable extinction, each generation of humanity commits to striving for perpetuity of the species, only in harmony with the universe. The right to life, liberty, and the pursuit of happiness in a society results from social intercourse, and the link between religious influence on human rights and commerce was palpable throughout the second millennium. Religious adherence increased with rising poverty, barbarous acts, and tainting of commerce, and it was striking and provocative. If the touch points were less frequent among these preemptive elements for conflict, the refuge of faith would not become a substitute for solving real problems of human rights, thereby avoiding religious wars.

SECTION VI: PROSELYTIZING

Homogenizing religion reduces the discordant preoccupation with the proselytizing.

FIRST AMENDMENT

Interpersonal, international, and intergenerational communications must give voice to the limitations of an unassisted human mind. Artificial intelligence is the only means of strengthening the marrow of humanity, and imagination is the only window to avoid annihilation.

SECTION VII: AFTERLIFE PROMISES

Homogenizing religion will not require prayer or sacrifice, human or animal, for a promise of afterlife felicities and perfection.

FIRST AMENDMENT

Pertinacious adhesions to lifeless images obliterate rational and vigorous knowledge essential to survival plans of humanity. Abandonment adds much to human happiness and unencumbered imagination needed for human dominion.

SECTION VIII: MIRACLES AND IMAGININGS

Homogenizing religion still encourages belief in miracles, visions, and extraordinary occurrences that emanate from real-time experiences.

FIRST AMENDMENT

Artificial intelligence that enhances human thinking is neither a bag of bolts nor digital chips. Often, it appears in the form of a universal dream, which is a natural occurrence, and one that is realizable when we reach a prescribed, but unknown, level of higher knowledge collectively. This powerful supercharge of knowledge from past human experiences, when used, constitutes all the knowledge in the universe available to us.

SECTION IX: UNIFYING CULTS

Homogenizing religion recognizes that human unification begins as cultish but ends in human singularity.

FIRST AMENDMENT

Whereas unifying the world to achieve a common goal is problematical due to diverse cultures, it is agreed that the addition of artificial intelligence is essential to coalescing humanity to prevent extermination. Be it resolved that Watson, or its quantum iterations, at a minimum, actively participate in further homogenizing diverse superstitions.

SECTION X: TRANSPARENCY

Homogenizing religion is manifestly transparent.

FIRST AMENDMENT

Whereas people with hidden beliefs always seek out willing sympathizers with whom to associate and compete for fame, be it resolved that genuine transparency and social intercourse are the best antidotes to relieve human stress and avoid violence.

SECTION XI: SACRED MUSIC

Homogenizing religion favors forces of musical expressions replete in the harmonics of the cosmos and tuned to living.

FIRST AMENDMENT

Whereas the music of the universe, like the sounds of Earth's oceans, empathize with the collective psyche of generations, be it resolved that all music is temporal.

SECTION XII: COSMIC RECOGNITION

Homogenizing religion is mankind's encounter with the cosmic membrane of cognition, the everlasting and only extraterrestrial contact ever.

FIRST AMENDMENT

Be it resolved that mankind, together with the support of AI, will ensure its survival by ending the violence of religious wars and embarking on an expedition to provide its descendants with the knowledge to overcome other threats of extinction.

PART III

FIVE HUNDRED YEARS LATER

WHAT THE WORLD LOOKS LIKE

TURNING POINTS

A host of turning points became the tipping point. The influence of homogenizing religion on humanity was more powerful than all scientific, social, legal, or military doctrines combined. Since the beginning of time, until the year 2539, the course of human events turned on one phenomenon in a single year. It liberated generations to live free from superstitions and other imagined fears. Ancient discoveries had contributed in fragments, but none could match the unshackling of people as did homogenizing religion. The steam engine, electricity, internal combustion engines, aircrafts, computers, and the internet didn't answer the fundamental intrigues of life, the earth, and the universe as well as homogenized religion did. Even at that time, in 2539, they had no idea about the nature of matter, the cosmos, consciousness, time, intelligence, and the purpose of life. This radical rupture between reality and perception can be attributed to generations of wasted lives, resources, and property to fight religious wars until the first universal dream of human enlightenment occurred in the year 2014 in the third millennium. There was an evolutionary change of human behavior and eventual understanding of who caused it and why.

Through half of the third millennium, society at large realized that no deity will ever save humanity, so it must save itself. The reaction to this new reality diverted scientists from the common stream of iterative products and inventions that produced massive profits in consumer goods to long-term, gigantic, macroscientific products. They rushed to outdo one another at warp speed by employing hypertechnology. Benefits from worker robotics, artificial intelligence, smart devices, and nanotechnical medical breakthroughs in genetics and quantum physics bypassed the customary metrics to enhance living standards. Artificial intelligence stocks soared while the economics of society at large patiently awaited the outcome of these futuristic, and often failed, utopian ventures.

The collective benefits of diverting vast intellectual and financial assets freed by homogenizing religion were thus pried from society's everyday needs. It was time for another reminder to cure mankind's ancient but often corrosive habit of rushing to profit when change is sensed by risk-takers. Blinded by a short life span, opportunists too often justify the herd instinct of human behavior as reason enough to act swiftly and deadly, until homogenizing religion proved the scope of acting on blind instinct has its limitations. This was the case until geoclonologists reached beyond the limitations of the human life span of three score and ten to millions of years of time needed to fully understand the context of hominin evolution following the extinction of all life on Earth. *Homo sapiens* evolved a level of cognition that enabled them to survive other threats, unlike prior life-forms. If only dinosaurs could think.

The human race faced extinction from self-inflicted violence in AD 2014, arising from the fanaticism of 4,200 religions—each of which rejected reality for a different doctrinal cause, usually without a distinction, which sent competing beliefs into the howling fires of hell, while ruining the lives of followers by having them fear the mystery of their very own existence. Our forefathers overcame it by rational thinking, courage, and imaginative dreams to restore cognitive thinking. Now, once again, in AD 2539, their descendants faced a problematic future caused by unforeseen consequences of their ancestor's resoluteness. They were aided by artificial intelligence that superseded human intellect. AI had the wherewithal to collect, sort, and process factual data without limitation, and the universal dreams helped to accurately channel and devise solutions to avoid annihilation. The universal dream mechanism, albeit inexplicable, was a fail-safe to avoid repeating the price of unintended consequences. At least that was how the people on Earth perceived it.

A new quid pro quo was beginning. Artificial intelligence was needed to enable the human species to survive, but survival of mankind meant serving a machine.

THE WORLD ORDER

The seventeenth generation of world leaders, since the adoption of the feasibility report, gathered at the latest iteration of the United Nations, now known as the United Regions (UR), in AD 2539 to discuss the progress of the feasibility report adopted in AD 2124 and implemented in AD 2139 as the decisive method to save humanity. Its careful implementation by past world leaders had already produced some impressive accomplishments.

The UR was housed in a single building that rose five hundred stories high, colloquially referred to as the mother of all silos, and was located in the naturally hard rock foundation of New York City. Within its interior, individual seats ascended from a main podium on the lowest kernel to the very top. Presentations were seamlessly translated through a maze of viewing screens and speakers beyond anything imagined when the project was conceived in AD 2014. The worldwide shock of global warming had long since gone, and oceans leveled off at a ten-foot rise from carbon pollution, in addition to a mean temperature increase on the sun of one-half degree. Attention turned toward land reclamation from the sea and a perfected process of seeding clouds to increase wind velocity and rainfall. Planning and methodology advanced each century to harmonize AI with human and robotic forces that together evolved into pillars to drive the societal transformation process needed for the long-term survival program that began five hundred years before. Politically, the Planet Visionary Innovation Agency (PVIA) of UR became a think tank charged with identifying, extracting, and implementing key themes from the convergence of these seismic challenges and adapting them to the constantly changing needs of humanity, including augmenting legions of people with artificial intelligence to become smarter, stronger, and more capable while expanding their empathy.

The chief planetary architect, Dr. M. Nimbastrat, addressed the world leaders, "During the past five hundred years, we have ushered in a number of augmentation apps that propel people with heightened capabilities to the tasks needed for our preservation plan. These augmentation methodologies included implanting subdermal chips to unlock digital passwords, on a need to know basis, with the wave of a hand. We have also administered genetic editing that eliminates inheritable diseases and enables thought processing that is faster and can interface with brain machines. These advances were achieved by constant emphasis on behavioral consciousness, a focus on familial and social mores of empathy and personalization and telepathic transference, all of which is needed for us to exist on an overpopulating planet. Our existential risk is manifested in the chaotic changes in the biosphere, a cosmic organism that encircles the earth from a depth of six miles below sea level to a height of five miles above it. This network encompasses all forms of life on Earth, which together we know as our world. However, the resources needed to sustain life within this thin layer are finite and unable to accommodate the unintended consequences of homogenized religion, which was the very cause of the first environmental convulsion.

"Industrially, as we try to separate human society from savior robotics, overseen by Watson, our smart factories and revolutionary technologies will collaborate with enhanced human skill sets to meet the needs of the plan as well as preserve the humane values of living in a civilized society." He continued, "The value of PVIA was demonstrated when the dilemma arose concerning the need to change humanity's circadian rhythm imbedded since the species began. Faced now with annihilation, customary sleep patterns collide with the essential timetable depicted in the feasibility report and adopted a priori. Notwithstanding numerous discussions in multiple world forums about the import of spending no less than one-third of our day asleep, it was generally concluded that the amount people slept emanated from our ancient agrarian culture and was now an obstacle to gaining the knowledge, production, and modernization needed to meet our current challenge. The eight-hour syndrome, derived from the oscillations of solar light and darkness, and heretofore deemed natural to all Earth's species, could be better controlled, under the circumstances, by orbiting artificial suns that would eliminate darkness.

"Having fully debated changing sleep habits of humanity," he continued, "and by extension, eventually all other mammals, Watson, the receptacle of all human knowledge, opined when prompted that radical alterations to humans were needed for simple telepathy, which, as you know, has already been perfected and is readily available. The changes are also needed for uploading thoughts or dreams that can expand an individual's knowledge database and, if prescient, memorialized and further used to control working robots that require neither light nor darkness to function twenty-four days, seven days a week. Therefore, more radical disruptions to human social systems can thus be permanently avoided in keeping with the spirit and purpose of the treaty for human survival."

Dr. Nimbastrat concluded his introduction, "It should also be noted that physical death is no longer an impenetrable barrier to the living with the advent of heretofore unknown, yet ever-present, Paraspermya."

Rising slowly from his stately office space, the Rt. Honorable Alewrites Molucanna, world secretary of Governance for Human Safety and Health, restated, "We need to ensure the quality of human life in perpetuity regardless of all challenges to survival that could arise. Our highest priority is to prove to each generation that living life is worthwhile." He continued, "The quality of human life will always be directly dependent upon an environmental philosophy that recognizes and preserves aesthetic values, qualities, and experiences with particular attention to avoid the gap between art and science. These are the principal premises for retaining the reality of self-regulated social communities during changing times as we lean more on technology to preserve our society.

"Our focus must not exclude the effects of art and culture, both exclusive human qualities of pleasure that make life worthwhile. Technology already serves us in many different and crucial ways, including an assurance of continuity 'life on a chip' methodology that prevents disease and suspends the nucleotides of MinION, thereby guaranteeing familial lines forever. The power of technology must always be heavily involved in genetic engineering to suppress the limitations and flaws in human reasoning and continuously improve our species by craving to blend science and art, each a distinctive quality of human life."

Molucanna departed temporarily from an intense focus to muse with a starry-eyed glaze, "This can become a golden age in human history wherein each person is content with what they have and no one prefers any possessions of another, where nobody is expert in inflicting wounds upon another, wherein modesty, love, honor, probity and beauty reign. This then is what humanity strives toward as we dedicate our efforts every day to survive. This is a right and is the nature of humanity, just as surely as gravity is a law of physics that governs water to run downhill. When happiness fails us, the purpose of our very existence is lamentable. Human satisfaction is not a laughing matter since it is the only antithesis to our afflictions of worry and pain."

Professor Labella Scaevala, the world's leading authority on the philosophy of knowledge, its acquisition, usage, transference, and storage, leaped from his seat and strove at a quickstep to the podium to deliver his long-awaited progress report on the status of collective human knowledge. Scaevala was physically short, wide, and fat but taller than most in intellect. His tie askance, jacket too tight, hair uncombed and flowing from the top of his bulbous head to his waistline as he addressed the assemblage, "Predicting collective knowledge five hundred years after homogenizing religion took hold is vastly different from quantitatively assessing the state of human knowledge five hundred years beforehand. Discerning fact from fiction isn't a task that is linear, geometric, or exponential like Moore's law would have it, but is basically a never-ending random search. Thanks to the advent of artificial intelligence, however, we can now instantly collect it in abundance, and confirm, adapt, and preserve it as a primary source and make it instantly accessible to all. Our existence depends on collective knowledge of all the sciences and appreciation of differing social cultures, the latter equally important to quality of life. This is strictly a human shared by all. For example, while Watson can't replicate the *Mona Lisa* for everybody to see and enjoy, humanity continues to cultivate a wide range of emotions, music, and many other art forms crucial to our existence."

Professor Scaevala stabbed the air with his forefinger and bellowed, "Knowledge is more than information processing! We believed there are no upper limits to it that can't be surpassed but now know they are only enhanced. And through the cogent and perpetual use of human endeavors, artificial intelligence, and Watson, we can constantly update and preserve 99.9 percent of all human knowledge. The remaining 0.01 percent we retain as an off switch to maintain our dominion over machines." He continued while mussing his shock of cloud-white hair, "The advances made in harnessing and managing knowledge would lead one to believe no further research on methodology is needed to establish fixed parameters for acquiring, confirming, aggregating, and applying it to every imaginable situation. That is not so! Our ancestors battled with the reality that new knowledge brought forward over two millennia via giant gatherers of knowledge, such as Plato, Zhuang Zhou, Buddha, and many others, all insinuating at one time or another that reality of new knowledge is illusionary and beyond the capacity of human intelligence and perception. It is beyond speculation today that only advanced thinking is capable of altering our perception of reality and that we make our world what we think it should be."

In a true professional manner, Professor Scaevala paused to sip some water, regroup, and let the doubt he posited sink into his captivated audience. He then continued, "Recently some of my colleagues believe they uncovered strong evidence that our three-dimensional human reality was a hologram of two-dimensions. They colluded by passing back and forth vast amounts of data on background radiation emanating from the big bang, using Watson's processing powers to couple these anomalies with existing quantum theory, and concluded that a two-dimensional holographic reality likely exists, and all we see are human illusions. Watson has yet to endorse that theory.

"It is important to understand how our approach to new knowledge has advanced in the five-hundred-year span between adopting the feasibility report and today. The standards for elevating a scintilla of data to a level of primary knowledge by the intelligence of Watson is of profound significance to our comprehension and, ultimately, to the quality of our life on Earth. Because time is of the essence, our primary goal is not to waste time with abstract theories and endless inquiries, but to function within as pure a knowledge discipline as possible to correct or discard knowledge imperfections. It was long held that the ultimate purpose of acquiring knowledge was to improve mankind's ability to predict the future. However, without control of it, there is little use for equating prediction with understanding, the latter being crucial today to our survival. How long it took for mankind to realize that the few lawful, orderly, and therefore predictable events that rose above the chaos of innumerable variables to get there was astonishing. This dichotomy permeates the universe and human behavior as well. In this instance, the negative proves that there is a positive need for us to collaborate with artificial intelligence, and Watson, to progress along the path of the feasibility report towards our survival as a species."

He continued gesticulating. "The two absolute challenges for us can be realized by accumulating primary source knowledge is to learn how to calculate the incalculable, and to comprehend the unknown unknowns so we may cogently deal with infinity itself! Without artificial intelligence and Watson, however, we are forever limited to looking back in history for knowledge borne by experience. Any notion that knowledge is static, like a single musical chord, was imagined from time to time but never entertained throughout the ages. We can't see the future despite our keen eyes and sense of change, but in the final analysis, we suffer from change blindness because our brains can only manage so much input and will naturally prioritize it. That is why we can't feel the clothes we wear or don't hear outside noises as we read. We rely on past experiences to fill the gaps and can't begin to tackle a multigenerational existential project without AI and Watson. These allegories challenge our notion of what reality is. Perhaps it is an illusion with which we have no choice but to agree.

"Humanity remains caught between an unknown beginning and an unimaginable end, and we can't escape those parameters. It's as though they haunt us. Five hundred years into our irrevocable survival plan, the scope of our limitations is problematic, so we turn to AI and Watson for achievements we can never attain alone. But we are human and, even when facing extinction, see fit to entrust our most essential creation with 99.9 percent of all human knowledge yet withhold 0.01 percent for the off switch. This is how humanity weighs caution against innovative speed and thereby defines, for all times, the relationship between humans and artificial intelligence. Broadly speaking, we are imparting all available knowledge to an advanced machine to enhance it sufficiently to help us survive an expected apocalypse. To do that, we must exercise our new superintelligence to decide myriad problems at lightning speed while performing everyday discrete tasks.

"We can never again afford to place our trust in a higher power whom we can't interrogate. Our forefathers learned that over five hundred years ago. The alternative is not simple, however, as Watson is trained by data, which infers answers, care must be taken not to experience 'garbage in, garbage out.' A simple artificial intelligence system can't be expected to always behave intelligently, while a system too complicated won't be understood if infused with human skepticism. We are still playing with fire as the legendary Prometheus, patron of dangerous discoveries, did ages ago, because the alternative is extinction."

After a twenty-minute recess, the professor continued, "I estimate the annual increase in human knowledge to be plus or minus 5 percent compounded, thereby adding new knowledge to humanity at 130 times per century. Assuming I am marginally accurate, humanity acquired new knowledge of six-hundredfold since the feasibility report was adopted five hundred years ago. However, along the way, some of that knowledge became obsolete, perhaps a case of truth decay. The knowledge we learned has a varied lifespan. In medicine and science, facts appear to have a fifty-year, half-life, or attrition rate that if applied to all other knowledge, it significantly reduces the six-hundredfold increase. Futuristically, the use of Watson quantifies all new knowledge at the speed of light to render the prospect of truth decay de minimis. Previously, knowledge was a function of possible choices, but today, such designation, while rare, is not a function of human pondering when resolved in nanoseconds by backing the dilemma into Watson, with an obviously wrong answer first backing into truth, if you will.

Five hundred years later, the unknown unknowns surround dark matter and energy, which together equals 95 percent of the universe, along with trillions of suns and planets. By the next five hundred years, our aggregate knowledge will advance by two-thousandfold to address these problems. Who knows, at that expectant rate, we might learn everything about anything, everywhere. Truly an excitatory future."

The audience erupted into deafening applause. As their cheers died down, the next speaker took the stage.

"I am pleased to announce that the digital recombinant transfer [DRT] of mobile computerized objects [MCO] is in an advanced state of a work in process. To those less familiar with these terms, our work on robotics has experienced major breakthroughs," bellowed Dr. Rava Cirrocumulus, EE, PhD, a world-renowned physicist, engineer, and robotic designer, who, as a fanatical feminist, stands four feet two inches and never uses a microphone— she claims they're for men and robots.

"Ironically," she exclaimed, "our ancestors chose the best path possible for the survival of humanity by their foresight in a future that would require virtual reality and reality to become synonymous and overcome natural evolution—the only discipline they knew. Today, robotics are ubiquitous and engineered to enhance our chance for surviving. They are not killing us as many feared. By virtue of artificial intelligence, and Watson, anything that anyone has ever done to benefit society is permanently recorded and instantly available for reuse. Watson does have a secret, and you will learn about that later. Our lives, meanwhile, are enhanced by our durability to conceive, plan, and enhance our ability to execute the multigenerational and mammoth feasibility report with which we will again defeat a threat of extinction to our species without sacrificing the newly homogenized culture of peace and happiness our ancestors strove to achieve for us some five hundred years ago. The degree of technical innovation we devised to assure progress in our time and for future generations will enhance life as we marshal our resources toward the final solution of our salvation.

"We have spent five centuries learning to be content, but now, unintended consequences radically alter our plans to stay at home! Although we are relieved from the daily herculean tasks before us— for which we were never suited—we can focus on the measures of contentment with which music, dance, and arts provide. Due to the generational sacrifice of blood, time, and treasure in artificial intelligence and superhuman robotics, everything we need travels to and from us at the speed of light, yet we have raw human emotions to contend with and still need clocks to tell time. This is a typical human dichotomy."

The audience roared with laughter and applause.

Dr. Rava, as she was reverently referred to, resumed her bellowing, "Until recently, say a century or two ago, AI and robotics were employed by us to relieve the tedium of repetitive tasks, a programmatic no-brainer that lulled us by obfuscating the mosaic of complicated tasks requiring copious monitoring and adjustments by Watson in order to stay the course of the survival plan. For example, the oversight needed to harness the sheer brute force used to alter the planet ranges in one instance from a standard atmospheric pressure at sea level of 15 psi to a hydraulic cutting force of 100,000 psi. This is not new to us, but to construct a robotic lifting strength of 10 million psi requires fail-safe designs and constant monitoring of digitalized high energy, hydraulics, and electromagnetic forces for each of a million individual MCOs, better known as robots, since the twentieth century. After adopting the feasibility report, the Fourth Industrial Revolution began and included collateral robots that specifically function in given environments like space and aquatics and housing construction and demolition. For example, they provide thirteen thousand new high-rise buildings per day to shelter five hundred thousand newly homeless occupants but using materials conveyed by heavy lift drones twenty-four-hours a day, seven days a week.

The advances in robotics were palpable to meet the magnitude of infrastructure support for a rapidly growing population. Despite that, tasks requiring judgment, like picking ripe bananas from a bunch, still requires a human touch. But that, too, changed by breakthroughs during the most recent century, providing new pathways for Watson to instantly deliver commands of contextual knowledge to robots with pinpoint accuracy about specific chores, objects, and environments. Known as comtext, a series of programming methods that marry exoskeletal robotic strength with intricate visual and spoken commands activate episodic memory banks [EMB] to respond instantaneously using digital inference reasoning [DIR] to execute the most copious tasks."

Poking the air above her with her forefinger, she reverted to rapid talk, "The comtext methodology of transference was tested only a century ago in the Antarctic, when the ice blanket was 2.5 miles thick and glaciers of potable water from core-heated subglacial lakes were transported for storage in the world's low-lying landmasses for use by the explosive population resulting from homogenizing religion five hundred years ago. This immense project required both enormous strength and quantum movements by an advanced AI component of Watson robotics to dislocate glaciers from the bed they languished in for half a million years. That is a remarkable achievement, more of which will be required by robotic engineering for DRT of mission-specific functions described in the feasibility report. These are accomplished by downloading cartridges of Watson's acquired knowledge and bypassing the slower learning process of teaching people.

"Ironically," she shouted after catching her breath, "AI robotics are essential to us because of our human limitations, but are designed to emulate our natural systems. Lifelike robots that learn and adapt are now ubiquitous, thanks to the engineering process of embedding computers in soft robotic-suited materials using conductive receptors to transfer and translate instructions in a plasma encompassing the entire body. Taking its inspiration from human biology, soft-skinned robots mimic the vascular system to disperse hormones, and enzymes are dispersed and detected by receptors to trigger appropriate responses. The state of robotics today is smart and autonomous once they are set to a task by Watson. The robots have evolved to a level of adapting to their immediate environment while providing us with the diversity of almost normal behavior coupled with superhuman strengths.

"For example, the neuromorphic region of Watson can transfer artificial synapses with digital electronics to support intelligence for individual robots that solve myriad problems as they occur on the spot. Robotic performance is markedly enhanced when processing. Transfer and storage occur on sight by standardizing core data wherever possible. Programming is faster, and energy output is less, allowing for replication in 1 billion worker-robots to meet our big project demolition and construction needs.

"Such is the status of engineered AI and robotics on this five hundredth anniversary!" she said. "And to that end, we must admire the Maecenas of Watson, because long after the evolution of the DNA molecule used to store the genetic code used by every life-form on Earth, we humans learned to repurpose its methodology to store factual data we uncover at an exponential rate. Watson is our version of DNA. Visualize the analogy between natural DNA and Watson. Both are open, awaiting input, storage, recall, collating, verification and codifying, and rearranging and purifying voluminous and continuous data, not to mention applying them on demand. Both require significant energy on call always to ensure integrity and precision for eons. A single gram of DNA contains 455 exabytes of data and 100 trillion meters all strung together to guarantee accurate replication. Even at Watson's advanced stage to manage this organized chaos, all human DNA would require a millionfold increase in processing capacity. Watson's machine capacity today can read millions of DNA sequences simultaneously while managing all other notable functions we depend on. That is nothing to sneeze at!"

The audience laughed again.

Rava continued, "This extraordinary machine capacity emanates from the mastery of nanotechnology that relies on physics and chemical engineering breakthroughs realized during the five hundred years since adoption of the report. This advanced methodology replaced data bits with DNA markers that fit one terabit of factual data known to the world, in a square inch of hard drive. The physics and engineering for artificial intelligence makes possible the one chance to save humanity. Such enhanced intelligence enables breakthroughs heretofore beyond human comprehension. For example, developing and applying a microchip tissue nanotransfection [TNT] that isolates any human cell requiring medical treatment while remaining in a patient's own body can repair, rejuvenate, and revitalize aging organs, vessels, or nerves by injecting genetic code through the skin. Absent any other toxic medication, it has increased the average human lifespan by twenty years and forever changed the biology of demise. I challenge anyone to contest what you heard here today!"

As she turned on her tippy toes like a ballet dancer and strutted away, the jaw-dropping silence was palpable.

Approaching the podium with lengthy, slow steps, arms dangling, eyes fixed on his shoe tops, spine bowed, and dressed in a wrinkled seersucker suit, Professor P. Cottonball Nimbus announced, in a gravelly voice, "I am the Energy Czar!"

The audience's laughter filled the room.

Obviously somewhat of a humorous foil, Dr. Nimbus began, "I am immersed in researching a new phase of coalescing enough energy to exercise dominion and control over our global climate. It can also be used to farm the oceans, enlarge habitable landmasses, transport data, images, audio, and more by the speed of light, and last but not least, to explore the universe without generating nuclear waste! We, oddballs, rank these tasks as advancing a type one civilization on the Kardashev scale, designate it an earth/sun driven system of renewable energy of five plus order of magnitude, higher than any ever attained before on Earth but nothing compared to channeling the sun's radiation, the energy and luminosity of which could destroy the planet. There is plenty of luminosity in the cosmos other than our sun, which, to date, is not contained by our planet or our universe."

The audience gasped as Dr. Nimbus quantified the magnitude of endless energy needed to execute the survival plan, anxious about where and how it would ever be achieved. Having this international congregation on the edge of their seats, the unassuming but illuminating Dr. Nimbus continued his presentation, "The fact is, and this is confirmed by Watson, that our massive energy needs to survive have no earthly equivalent or source equal to the task we face. Not nuclear fusion, cold fission, reflective solar satellites, black hole siphoning, or energy siphoned from white holes. Yes, there are white holes in the universe. Yet our need for a permanent super-energy link surpasses any limits known even from quantum particle collisions or any other source. You are probably wondering what we are going to do."

The audience sat quietly, mesmerized, waiting for his solution.

Dr. Nimbus did not disappoint them. He shouted, "I have an answer from generations of merging copious research and experiments with artificial intelligence and the latest iteration of Watson. We finally mastered an iconic process to protect dielectrics from any known harsh heat environment by pairing a one-dimensional, nanocomposite polymer with a two-dimensional element of boron nitrate. The result is a super-dispersal heat shield that protects against extremely hot plasma created by the intense flow of electrons of 1.4 billion flashes of lightning that land on Earth each year. Now we can harness these celestial electromagnetic radiations and produce an unlimited, nonpolluting, and permanent energy force capable of meeting any of our human needs. We perfected the process known as fulminology."

A heckler emerged from somewhere in the audience and said, "Dr. Nimbus, will we need a kite with a key on a string or a lightning rod to bottle some of this energy?" The audience reacted with laughter.

Professor Nimbus was unfazed. "Ha, ha, you might try it though, when you are alone," replied the good-natured Energy Czar, his well-camouflaged brilliance shined as he continued to impress new knowledge upon his captive audience. He continued, "Each cloud-to-ground lightning strike is a natural plasma channel to Earth that emits thirty thousand to a hundred thousand amperes of energy per microsecond, and as mentioned earlier, it occurs 1.4 billion times each year, mostly in the tropics. With the new material extractors to harness, store, and direct any of these powerful shock waves of super-heated expanding air molecules, Watson can instantaneously route raw electricity to a controlled collection grid that disburses it exactly as needed by anyone, and it can do it forever!"

En masse, the UR participants arose and applauded the advances sighted by Dr. Nimbus to assure an evergreen source of energy for mankind in the five hundred years since the world adopted the feasibility plan for its survival.

But Dr. Nimbus was not yet through presenting. After acknowledging the audience's appreciation, he waved them to be reseated while shouting, "Wait, there's more!" Then he continued, "Despite the breakthrough enabling us to harness lightning as a permanent energy source for the world, there are more challenges to address, as in the vast landmass required for the grid and transfer sites needed to disburse the encapsulated energy to where and when it was needed. Land usage is desperately needed for human habitation facing an exponential population explosion, which, after all, is the existential consequence of homogenizing religion. To use it elsewhere is antithetical. The solution rests in, of all things, origami. Among Watson's research and development designs, origamic algorithms were developed to fabricate grids by printing all materials and electronic components that are deployable to transmit energy on demand with the speed of light to great distances. Once arrived, these compactions explode like fireworks into incalculable subchannels of demand. Absent these origami enabling algorithms of distribution, the power grid would occupy a thousand times the amount of space."

The UR audience gasped in unison at the unimaginable achievement of locating and managing super-energy sources so vital to humanity.

Dr. Nimbus continued, "But wait, allow me to inform you of the collateral application of fulminology that prepares the way for humanity to travel to the stars!"

With hands on their heads, mouths wide open, and eyes straining at their sockets, the listeners reseated themselves en masse.

The professor cleared his throat, sipped some water that dribbled down onto his shirt and tie, and lunged into a tirade. "Until now, deep-space travel relied on electric propulsion to power engines that shot rockets up to twenty times faster than traditional fossil fuels while those aboard instantly communicated with Earth using mental telepathy. Their conveyance was stuck in a rut, first conceived back in the twentieth century. Now, with the advent of dispersal heat shields and the new science of fulminology, we unshackled the forces of inertia to propel objects into and throughout space. Basically, when an object accelerates, its energy emissions change the mass, and the resulting shape is warped by resistance of dark energy, the antithesis of dark matter, to its unparalleled speed. The changed anatomy of the now-charged object affects its inertia and how it relates to the rest of the ambient universe when propelled by high-density voltage to a warp speed of light. Even after the voltage supplied by lightning subsides, it is ready to be called on again and again as needed from an inexhaustible supply stored continentally and drawn upon by an almost invisible grid of pods tuned by microwaves.

"My job is to energize an unprecedented and advanced standard of living for all humanity every day for a thousand years, during which the feasibility report for survival of humanity is implemented. We are assisted and abetted by a level of artificial intelligence never known to mankind before this. Thanks to the latest iterations of Watson, we are able to do this from extraterrestrial sources without any pollution by tapping a billion years of inexhaustible energy emanating directly from the main engine that drives the universe. Modern physics and artificial intelligence render it incontrovertible that celestial energy abounds all about our space vehicle called Earth.

"Thank you for the opportunity to report on the status of energy in the five hundredth year since approval of the feasibility report," said Dr. Nimbus who, with clasped hands held high above his frazzled hair, retired stage left.

The audience stood, applauded enthusiastically and more.

Ensconced in a floor-length black burqa as she approached the podium, international land architect Madam Annona Muricata exclaimed, "Unlike my colleagues who preceded me, the future of my project has arrived! The short-term aspect of our existential undertaking is completed and, as I speak to you today, is functioning as planned and providing sustenance and shelter to the expanding citizenry of our planet. Spatial recycling of human interment practices that occurred daily over three millennia no longer exists, and the land reserved for cemeteries worldwide has been recaptured to serve only the living.

"The term *reductionism* was heretofore reserved to describe the physics of life-science complexities. Today the acceptable etymology includes spatial recycling. The feasibility report adopted five hundred years ago by our ancestors for survival of our species stated that more of the 2 million square miles of Earth's surface is to be preserved for the exclusive province of life as we know it. Three hundred thousand square miles of land heretofore used to inter the dead were reclaimed as habitable land for the living. It occurred over a seventeen-year period and cost 17 trillion US dollars. This initial phase of the multigenerational survival plan was intended to provide a stop-gap solution of immediate benefits for the unintended consequence of the exponential population explosion of a war-free world of homogenized religion."

Lifting her delicate, lace-covered facial veil, Madam Muricata continued, "The short-term solution of reversing 5 billion interments was achieved as planned with mass human labor, employing artificial intelligence and Watson-managed robotics in record time and at one-half the projected cost, proving the intrinsic value of coordinating human effort with Watson. Today, five hundred years after adopting this action plan, the reclaimed land is inhabited by 3 million people, none of whom would be alive were it not for the intercession of our ancestors to homogenize religion."

Stripping off the outer layers of her burqa to reveal a flattering bikini from Victoria's Secret, which was still in business, Madam Muricata held it high so all could see and said, "But for discarding this canvas burqa, a world-renowned symbol of but one of 4,200 religions, neither I, nor any of you, would be here today. Kudos to our ancestors for homogenizing religion." Then she sashayed away from the podium.

THE UNKNOWN UNKNOWNS

A WORD ABOUT ALIENNUS

Dr. Ciro Undulatus, better known among his peers as the Dream Merchant, began a presentation with an allegory of neurolinguistics of this latest millennium and how we parsed and probed our brains in order to close the vast evolutionary gap between frenzy and cognition by defining what limits the human brain can reach in the fundamental sense, thereby defining us as conscious beings by virtue of a sprawling network of 100 billion neurons housing 100 trillion synapses.

The Dream Merchant began by saying, "Today, Watson's latest iteration successfully reproduced this vast network as a unified one, and it's meant to clarify cognitive thoughts and suggested that mind abstractions, like dreams, result from a malfunctioning neural circuitry. More work, however, is required to quantify this suspicion. We have long been aware that over a human lifetime, a small fraction of brain capacity is used to sustain life, but Watson proved our entire brain is always active in permanently assigned modulations not unlike a well-conducted orchestra playing inside our heads, awaiting an imputed scoring and tune." Stroking his well-groomed beard, Professor Undulatus continued, "How often have we spent a day pondering an imponderable, only to find a resolution upon waking the next morning? So frequent an experience that it appears nature provided us with a kind of perverse pleasure in reverse, whereby our consciousness seemed limited and problematical, but the fiction of a dream-state gifted us another dimension of insight to obtain the eluded answer, as though we conjured it into existence. From time to time in our history, we witnessed the anomaly of a universal dream, one that causes all living beings to dream the same dream at the same time, according to their circadian rhythms, and thus guide humanity toward what turned out to be the only solution to a problem of existential magnitude. Watson's archives are ripe with validated testimonials about these phenomena. Whether classified under perverse intrusions or consensual hallucinations, we are here today at the five hundred-year benchmark because of them."

A head-turning buzz arose from the vast crowd of listeners as a well-dressed, middle-aged person, between eighty and one hundred years of age, got up from his seat, placed his hand on his temple, and telepathized a question. "Professor, what is a consensual hallucination?" Everyone shook their heads approvingly.

Laughing out loud, Dr. Undulatus shouted, "All of you just participated in one! I just dropped the meme consensual hallucination, and a firestorm erupted among you to become better informed about it to the exclusion of everything else. A turn-of-art idea or phrase that captures the imagination of everyone is a consensual hallucination. Anything we take for granted is only real because we agree it is. The consolidated international legal system we live under is nothing more than multiple memes, influencing each culture on the planet disseminated by local law schools that we agree to participate in. Our worldwide economy consists of universally accepted memes of exchanging the value we place on the time, needs, and items. We then provide ourselves with a portion we choose to devote to make our lives worthwhile. The uniform methodology designed to expedite the process is called doing business, and those who function therein even have their own meme for failure called bankruptcy.

"But enough about the mnemonics of consensual hallucinations," said Dr. Undulatus. "As an expert in solipsism, I personally favor individual consciousness stimulated by memes and dreams. Humanity, to me, is the product of information processing by a single organ, the brain, most of which, thanks to Watson, meets our criteria for truth in perpetuity, subject to constant updating by us as we awake from a complex dream, upon which we decided to act and add the experience from a personal conscious phenomenon. At least, we like to believe our contribution bears a touch of individualism, something our ancestors were totally dependent upon. Some doubt remains, and the mystery of the genesis of new knowledge creation remains. Throughout history, there are numerous memes traced to inexplicable universal dreams that when acted upon changed to course of humanity. The ancients of five hundred years ago, upon experiencing this phenomenon simultaneously in each of thousands of languages, were both frightened and titillated to the extent of convening think tanks to eschew any obfuscation caused by human emotion to explain the inexplicable. Nothing helped explain a collective act that blindly changed the course of human behavior forever. We are still subject to living out its prophecy today, twenty-five generations later.

"During the modern era," he continued, "there are a plethora of universal dreams documented and codified, although not identified, under a banner of the unknown unknowns, a high-priority research and development project for Watson to solve. Recently, it is reported that the latest iteration of Watson's deep probe intrusion project beyond perceived reality [DPIP] caught a glimpse of how memes, and things like them, are discovered based on an assumption methodology that everything in the universe emerged from a single substance. In passing, the ancient Greek philosopher Plato toyed with similar notions way back in the first millennium, resulting in an often-repeated theory of ages that another unseen world exists beyond what we humans perceive. Absent actual proof, however, it never gained purchase and forever remained a mystery. Other's theories, such as presentism, externalism, abstracts of consciousness, multi-universes, etc., suffered the same end. The common denominator of all those abstractions was, and to some extent continues to be, mankind's search for the unknown unknowns.

"The research aspect of Watson operates on a plane different from the reality of gathering, verifying, continuously updating, and archiving of all human knowledge crucial for executing the feasibility report for survival. That advanced state of artificial intelligence recently sensed unusual spurts of thermal energy seemingly emanating from a swarm of particles moving at the speed of light among the dark matter, separating the organic matter of the Milky Way. Watson's DPIP posited that such unimpeded dynamics could only be explained by contracting and expanding ions of unidentified matter within its own construct, liking it to a swarm of locusts that appear to be growing larger with each sighting. The enormity of this discovery is remarkable but pales by comparison to the mystery of how detectable heat energy emerges from an absolute zero temperature environment of dark matter."

A din of chirps, tweets, musical notes, and chimes could be heard as the audience tried to assimilate this new data. Sensing the moment of surprise in an era so advanced that few occur, Dr. Undulatus continued, "Wait, there's more! Watson reports the plasma recombinant transfer mechanism [PRT] lights up like an ancient Christmas tree, indicating the presence of human life-forms. Also, the archived algorithms of past universal dream episodes appear to be related to Paraspermya, the identity now permanently ascribed to this new phenomenon."

Aware that five hundred years after adopting the report to save humanity, his every word describing the progression of the world's knowledge base was instantly transmitted to everybody of interest. Dr. Undulatus summarized the prospect of unraveling of an unknown unknown. He announced, "We are witness to, first, a swarm of particles traveling among the dark matter at the speed of light. Second, pulsations and heat that mimics the elements of life. And, third, a possible correlation between universal dreams and empirical knowledge."

This was jaw-dropping, shocking news for the world. The audience physically present at the hearing gasped in unison, and hands shot up to offer succor.

Dr. Undulatus waited for his words to sink in, and then continued, "Such an array of correlations, while awe-inspiring, don't explain causation, so let us pause to consider how to perceive them. That is, let's sleep on it and resume tomorrow."

Of course, the whole world was aware of his declared hiatus, and reactions ranged from acceptance to distrust of the possibility of a real alien contact. And it came to pass that every human being slept according to their personal circadian rhythm during which they experienced a nocturnal visit from the universal dream. The timing couldn't be better were it planned, which it wasn't. Humanity experienced in real time the sum and substance of Dr. Undulatus's exposé by living the dream they only imagined before Aliennus.

THE MOST COMPELLING DREAM IN FIVE HUNDRED YEARS

In REM state, everyone, everywhere, experienced this same dream on the same day:

The outer limit of mankind's ability to think and reason suffers from a common perception that extrapolates from a core assertion that nothing exists beyond consciousness, and all other anomalies, including memes, dreams, and abstractions, are just shades or imaginings of reality. Our ancestors fought over theories and prophecies for millennia, within 4,200 different religions, until acting on this, chaos threatened the collective existence of humanity. Aided by sublime encouragement that some thought hallucinatory, they homogenized religion over the course of a century to address the immediate threat. And it worked for them. There were, however, unintended consequences even more severe, with which we are still dealing today, five hundred years later.

Despite herculean efforts to corral and codify all human knowledge available to enhance our limited ability to deal with the second existential threat to human life, we sensed there was an even greater wealth of knowledge in the universe, and a stream of notions emerged in our search, each eventually were subsumed by another just as unfounded. Some of these are parallel universes, multi-universes, and the idea of eternalizing. Each one is a variation of the same theme, which was dispelled by Watson, our earthborn cistern of artificial intelligence. At this stage in our evolution, the evidence is now complete to everyone's satisfaction, including Watson's, and can be shared with you tonight. You are the first generation of mankind to know how the universe began!

Clearly it originated from nothing, but this particular nothing was embedded in a time dimension that endured through the transition of leaked quantum particles into the dark energy, a propellant of newly formed dark matter now part of the space-time past as the present was annihilated and the future became randomized. That randomized future birthed Earth, among other things. And the birthing of our planet unpredictably provided the elements necessary for life to form. This unchained evolution eventually left in its wake additions to the universal past in the form of the specific and cognitive human experiences we call Paraspermya! So the secret of how it all began doesn't lie in the big bang, string, or holographic theories. Instead, it is the knowledge that the future is determined solely by the collective cosmic past that began from nothing but the dimension of time, in keeping with the laws of physics as we know them today. And this future will continue to be exponentially fueled by a continuous annihilation of the present into the collective past, which in turn determines a randomized and otherwise unpredictable future. Paraspermya is but the latest and smallest addition to the space-time dimension but the end-all in the human quest for knowledge.

What we call Paraspermya was born not of man's imagination but discerned by the vast artificial intelligence of Watson to strain the outer limits of our collective minds, yet limited, these minds do not allow for the comprehension of the meaning of our existence. Alone, we will find it impossible to do, just as the ancients did before the seminal solution of homogenizing religion cured the uniquely human disorder of religious wars. Both the cause and remedy were products of universal dreams, the mystery of which were a source of worldwide speculation and cynicism for centuries.

Now, five hundred years hence, the discovery of heightened cosmic intelligence to further aid us begins the unraveling of an atavistic puzzle. But what is its construct? Is it older than the cosmos, or did it come into being in parallel with the emergence of the human species? What constitutes an energy source so powerful as to raise the intellectual prowess of humanity beyond anything imaginable and yet go unnoticed for millennia? Today, the living occupants of our planet may well have discovered, with the assistance of Watson, their own creation, the very secret of human life itself! Paraspermya is a force powered by every thought, meme, scrap of knowledge borne by every human being who ever lived to occupy Earth. It is the ultimate well of continuously refreshed wisdom that forever traverses the universe and is now available on demand to this generation and all that follows. Your dream tonight is shared simultaneously with every other living human, all who now know that by combining their evolutionary life with each other, guided by Watson, is conclusory in that we finally reached the outer limit of comprehension.

When you awake, the riddle of life no longer exists, and the mysterious driving force behind the feasibility report for survival, guided by dreams of cosmic intervention, is revealed for the very first time. When awake, any delusions harbored by you becomes de facto reality to a peaceful survival. Then, and only then, will I, Aliennus, ambassador plenipotentiary to planet Earth, return to Paraspermya. By then, your enduring desideratum will be codified by a manifesto humanus.

THE NEXT MORNING

Dr. Undulatus gaveled his group, and by proxy the whole world, to order the next morning. He faced a sea of raised hands, smiled, and began. "Yes, yes, it really happened to us! We are the first generation privy to factorial secrets of the dark universe absent any prerequisite to believing it was improvidently granted. Remember, our ancestors lusted after, and killed each other, to sequester their pernicious religious beliefs without the benefit of reality as we know it today. Their beliefs were supported by refreshing old superstitions from generation to generation, all illogical, poorly considered, and exhaustively filled with delusions. Eventually, the universal order via Paraspermya and Aliennus put a stop to it, the unintended consequences of which we are still dealing with five hundred years hence. Although the future is random and unpredictable, the good news is a dispositive understanding of the heretofore unknown unknowns is emerging with the help of advanced artificial intelligence, Watson, and the prime source of all wisdom in the allegoric universal dreams. By archiving this long-awaited scenario for future generations within a new manifesto humanus, the new age of factual thinking will remove our species from the endangered list."

A PROCLAMATION
HUMANUS FOR AD 2649

FOR PEOPLE OF THE EARTH

SECTION I: THE COSMOGENY OF SURVIVAL

The seminal answer to galactic chaos is human ingenuity and artificial intelligence.

The "start small, think big" strategy was a crucible of society for centuries, but when challenged with an overwhelming amount of evidentiary data gleaned from artificial intelligence, the approach changed. Development and coalescence of smart technologies that analyze and accurately predict the future conclusively augment human ingenuity and commoditize Aristotelian methods of problem-solving. We, the thoughtful on Earth, hereby adopt a mutual dependency approach as essential to our survival.

SECTION II: THE HUMAN POLYGLOT OF NATURE AND ARTIFICIAL INTELLIGENCE

Natural evolution is usurped by artificial intelligence.

In view of the multitude and enormity of the tasks facing us and future generations, it is no longer enough to focus on individual well-being from Darwinian laws. By adopting and expanding artificial intelligence, we harness technology to the longevity equation in a profound and sustained manner. Augmenting the human workforce ubiquitously with AI opens new avenues of value that were heretofore absurd in logic and pernicious in practice. The inflection points for this new collaboration include longer, healthier human lives coupled with superhuman robotic strengths that result in a 99.9 percent task reliability rating. Every age has benefited from progressive technologies. What makes this time unique is that for the first time every person is entitled to all of its benefits.

SECTION III: THE MOTHERBOARD OF ALL KNOWLEDGE

Paraspermya is the Maecenas of Watson.

The library of human thoughts began with the eve of humanity and proved to be a panacea of worldwide intelligence. By interfacing and employing the brain with Watson and Paraspermya, we can explain why time began and if it will end. We can understand the efficacy of the big bang and emergent hologram theories, all of which are crucial to the existential import of the human species. Also, on a more practical plane, wisdom, knowledge, and virtue must always be diffused among the people to preserve their rights and liberties. It is the duty of future generations to cherish literature and science and to support and inculcate their principles for the pleasure of all people.

SECTION IV: THE IMPORTANCE OF LIGHT AND DARKNESS

Eclipsed by a need to survive.

Circadian rhythms eclipse the need to sharpen expectations during periods of crisis since they are night extinguished, and our reality is sculptured mostly in daylight. Our waking lives would extend by one-third without preordained periods of sleep, thereby joining the never-resting cosmos. Artificial suns, precisely calibrated to smart robots, bridge the gaps between habit-formed human realities and an existential need for galactic cohesion.

SECTION V: CLONING

From sheep cells to digital recombinant replication.

The incentive attached to this methodology of replication is rescuing a species out of pending extinction by penetrating the nucleus of a single cell containing its genetic information. This mechanism for cloning is held in trust by all of humanity, as a last resort, to assure the diversity of life.

SECTION VI: A WORLD WITHOUT BORDERS

Universal dreams link the cosmos with humanity.

The great mystery that distinguishes humanity from all else in the universe is the vision of our mind's eye. The biology of a human visual cortex is dynamic when excited by sight, except when dreaming. Dreams, however visual they may seem, bypass the pathway through the pupils and flow directly to the mind's eye. What is dreamt is a hologram of hypnotic induction, but when streamed from Paraspermya, it is induced with added substance to an original thought, thereby attaining a high level of constructiveness to basic human understanding to create a confirmed source of new knowledge. We now recognize universal dreams as the anatomical, creative part of the human mind that is linked to the universe.

SECTION VII: COBOTS

The Fourth Industrial Revolution.

Domesticated animals, steam power, mechanization, and robotics were all developed to augment the limited productivity of people. Later on, artificial intelligence and smart robotics had a more substantive effect. As managed by Watson, the Fourth Industrial Revolution exceeded all other efforts to increase human productivity by a factor of three thousand times and human innovation by five thousand times. As a direct result, humanity prospered enough to house, clothe, care, and entertain every person for generations.

Artificial intelligence, consisting of digitized software and hardware, was capable of mustering superhuman strength. It assembled gigantic quantities of data, dissected, analyzed, and stored each morsel, and problems were solved on-site faster with a high degree of accuracy than humans ever could hope to achieve without it. The societal benefits derived from cobots that Watson controlled were crucial to the distinction between those of unique expertise who devoted themselves to executing the feasibility report for survival of humanity, and a society that needed a pliable and consistent economy to assure each generation that life is worth living while they await the final solution.

SECTION VIII: THE KNOWN UNKNOWNS

Surviving the known unknowns is a work in progress.

The feasibility report, adopted five hundred years before, commenced to recycle extant land for habitation and reclaim land from the sea and from recontoured mountains to support the burgeoning population. As the technology for these gigantic feats evolved, it was estimated that they would be completed within five hundred to one thousand years. During the interim, intergenerations patiently managed to function in a humane manner, knowing that their eventual survival depended upon emigration to other planets in the solar system. At the halfway marker, some of it remained a measurable work in process; some remained unsolved.

Also unsolved was the idea that time could be a dimension. Like many other cosmic antimonies, time emerged after the early universe was in a homeostatic state, and it was becoming clear that time was essential to measure the effects of cosmic bursts as they metamorphosized into triangles, rectangles, and other shapes they retain from then to today. Watson predicted further insights were highly likely to prove exactly why time began and why it could end. After all, time saved can't be stored and is contradictory to existence, in which time needs to be spent. Another known unknown.

Cosmic inflation was an enigma too. Setting aside the de facto origin of the universe, Watson's research to explain exponential growth began with reverse engineering each Earth day to determine the stability of its correlations with alike primordial elements. The reactions to each burst of exponential expansion, unlike a single big bang, allowed Watson to measure lifespans and annihilations, which provided energy for the next burst but found these quantum jitters to be the cause of cosmic microwave background noise. Next, this was tested against the ancient Heisenberg principle governing electrons and quarks. As the sole keeper of all human knowledge since time began, each iteration of Watson had run research in background for centuries to prove or disprove the big bang theory that persisted throughout the millenniums. By varying methodology from Aristotelian logic to recessive regressions, certain time-space benchmarks were established with certainty. For example, it became known that since 12.8 billion years ago, the universe looked much the same throughout time, although the expansion is slowing. Watson predicted with a high degree of certainty that the Stelliferous Era will end in 86 billion years. Stars will no longer form, and expansion will stop, but at that time, nothing was known about fate; and it seemed that there was no galactic order, just a chaotic transition to uncertainty. Everyone wondered if the answer would emerge with help from Paraspermya and Aliennus. Another known unknown.

PART IV

ONE THOUSAND YEARS LATER

THE NEW MILLENNIUM

MISSION ACCOMPLISHED

Aliennus returned to Paraspermya when the third millennium ended and when all human souls were permanently domiciled. The ancient's souls and newly arrived millennial billions were witness to the rare experience of hearing firsthand how completing a galactic assignment of one thousand earth years proved successful in saving an entire race of beings. Of course, looking back and knowing the outcome made for a better lesson than being present at the beginning. However, given the ephemeral nature of the environment and the transitory nature of the ever-growing population of souls, Aliennus created a library of telepathic dreamcasts for the populated galaxy, including Paraspermian souls and living humans, available from the Archives of Universal Dreams at Luna University. This ethereal library of truths was testimony to the nature and herculean effort of humanity to prevent their extinction. The dreamcasts also documented the myriad of unintended consequences that arose along the way and were dealt with by an intergenerational coalition, supplemented by successive advances in artificial intelligence, and guided even further by the induced dreamcasts of galactic knowledge proffered by Aliennus.

Telepathic dreamcasts were streamed to humans in a series of universal dreams for subsequent generations in perpetuity. Although complete, provisions were made for the dreams to include answers to thoughtful inquiries at the time of streaming. The methodology for accessing 100 billion brain neurons and penetrating the magnetoencephalography plasma grid to make this transference happen was imputed into the human genome by Aliennus sometime during the last quartile of the millennium.

This line of communication worked seamlessly between humanity and Paraspermya while people were in a dream-state. The catalyst server for storing this ubiquitous occurrence was the quantum iteration of Watson.

DREAMCAST 1—LOOKING BACK

Aliennus looked back at the third millennium and imparted the following dream:

> *This is the first of many dreamcasts originating from the ethers of Paraspermya, memorializing my thousand-year mission to help guide the fate of planet Earth. Despite the level of species' innate intelligence, boosted by artificial intelligence, more in-depth knowledge was required by multiple generations to avoid the extinction of the human species. Stopping the violent disruptions of religious wars was imperative to improve the dynamics of the universe. Looking back, it worked, but humanity was left with unintended consequences throughout the third millennium and required invisible guidance to remedy. At the time, earthlings were conclusively convinced of at least four basic truths:*

1. *Humanity is alone in the universe.*
2. *Dreamcasts can replace language.*
3. *The universe is flat.*
4. *All legendary gods were mythological.*

> *You are alone! There are no little green men, humanoids, lifelike abstractions, supermen, superwomen, or anyone else to talk to or visit with in the whole universe. Humans only have one another and come equipped with biological brains that only life on Earth can expand into human minds. Minds that concoct celestial contacts that will never come,*

construe superior beings beyond all reason, impute astounding intellect to anything different, and spend generations of precious time and treasure rehearsing for face-to-face meetings with all sorts of imagined creatures. The reality of universal life is, at best, growing a cabbage on some distant world or owning up to understanding and accepting the past, which is everlasting by always annihilating the present. However, your past assures nothing more than a randomized future.

Humanity exists alone in the cosmos, a creature of a common soul in a universe of distance, stone, and insensate matter. All this matter was created in the past, and humanity must look backward as the only reference for predicting the future. But it is a fool's journey, for while human brains are capable of gathering, storing, and recalling knowledge of the past, these most complicated objects in the universe beg the question of whether the mind it houses is flesh birthing cosmic knowledge or cosmic knowledge that birthed the flesh to contain itself.

With 86 billion neurons, no two are alike, yet all are connected to signal one another and thousands of others across 100 trillion synapses to create human consciousness—the fundamental wonder of all existence. From time to time, in a surge of self-confidence, some laws of physics that were always there are discovered and used to gain insight into a host of futuristic theories.

However, all that changed with the advent of artificial intelligence, which compounded information to create vastly improved iterations of Watson, and that name has become interchangeable with AI. A significant contribution to the development of Watson emanated from Paraspermya, the only comprehensive collection of ideas, thoughts, and knowledge in the universe from every human who ever lived on Earth. This seamless additive, delivered in universal dreams, enhanced the collective cognition of generations that heretofore only acquired knowledge from limited earthborn experiences.

My role, as an interventionist from Paraspermya, channeled an ultimate reservoir of knowledge to each living generation during their circadian sleep state for immediate use upon wakening. An ancient Earth philosopher, Friedrich Nietzsche, wondered, "If humanity's limited thinking was nature's blunder or was nature one of humanity's blunders?" Today, we realize the elusive cognition to inspire humanity to a higher mezzanine of knowledge was caused by timing. That inaccessibility to total cosmic knowledge was thwarted by an intergenerational mutation within the human species of a need to learn by first imitating ancestors, often resulting in wrong assumptions to build on.

A worldwide Truth and Reconciliation Commission was activated in the year AD 3700 to unlock the newly discovered mass of universal knowledge and, where necessary, reverse and repair any crippling precursory damage and foster an eruption of independent thinking that could neutralize irreversible elisions. And it worked!

Humanity's access to the dream program, which includes the new knowledge collective of Paraspermya, paved the way for coping with a variety of existential predictions. Intervention to mitigate or overcome them was never before possible, since some required multigenerational solutions; others needed centuries or a millennium to remedy. Until now, total reliance was on the natural processes of evolution built upon empirical earthborn evidence and random, disparate predictions of the future. Strangely, this limited approach proved to be complementary rather than contradictory to the added advent of Watson.

The other humanly intuitive sense to understand the forces at work encompassed equations and more abstractions to comprehend principles of reason. Together they served humanity with holistic, albeit temporary, explanations to muddle through a morass of exponential searches for a fail-safe predictive solution. Time proved a randomized future prescient. Some of the unsubstantiated predictions included Earth devolving into a frozen state or reality depending on individual consciousness or Earth made of a single substance. A parallel universe predictive theory declared the future was purely imaginary, reality is the past, and the present is only a phenomenon of consciousness—a guess eventually proved to be closest to reality.

QUESTIONS AND ANSWERS

The night after the dreamcast, there was further contact from Aliennus in response to questions that arose across the globe.

Good evening, earthlings. Thank you to those who responded to my first dreamcast with queries for further elaboration. To begin with, I have selected several topics of extreme interest to you, and reply to each in this dreamcast, as follows:

Two billion participants asked, "When did we know with certainty that we are alone in the universe?"

When the explosion of technology took part in the human need to communicate with one another to, among other things, encourage curiosity, imagination, reasoning, and conclude its dominance was made in the image of God. In that instance, the species morphed from one of distinction on Earth to one without a cosmic difference unless aided by artificial knowledge. The myopia of the human intellectual reach was always severely tested and limited by human emotion. The panoply of past human knowledge, however, was garnered by the vast swarm of humanity's only contribution to universe. Ever growing and constantly revolving around all cosmic regions as the Kuiper Belt and Oort cloud, suns, and planets, this came to be known as Paraspermya, the archive of all current human knowledge, to form a fail-safe capability to reach out to cosmic regions one thousand light years in radius with zero errors.

Indeed, humans and their thoughts are alone in the universe.

One billion participants asked, "Are dreamcasts so powerful a source of knowledge as to eventually replace language?"

Almost! Beginning in the twenty-first century of the third millennium, the engineers of data mining residing in North America's Silicon Valley of California declared their array of data-processing algorithms obsoleted the value of spoken languages and physical gestures that characterized human societies and whole civilizations founded on the meaning and value of words, including the very energy of human thought.

The central theme of radicalizing communication methodology was to rechannel the human experience and pleasures of biologically transferring knowledge among generations to the more efficient and time-saving digital means. However, it had the opposite effect. As their techniques coalesced in the limitless capacity of Watson iterative to test and retest until factuality was established by distilling data and until it was accepted as primary sources of knowledge or discarded, it failed to euphemistically shrink the cartridge of world knowledge and simultaneously stretch human minds.

You see, biological evolution alone proved to be an insufficient force to assure ever-increasing human intelligence and wisdom. It merely favored survival of the fittest by competition.

However, an infinitely plastic and perfectible human mind devised an artificial intelligence enhancement device to mesh with human needs. The only exception was the abundance of unworldly knowledge residing in Paraspermya. This archive was revealed to humanity by me when Watson completed collecting, confirming, and storing all present-day worldly knowledge. This layer of artificial intelligence rewound every scintilla of knowledge ever known into an exponential inflation of human understanding of how things work universally, as in the laws of physics. Those laws, and all other knowledge, are available to every living person from simultaneous dreamcasts from Luna University. About this, there is no debate.

Four billion participants asked, "Is the universe really one dimensional?"

A great question! The answer is yes. The observable universe from Earth appears as a spherical volume of space. According to Watson, it consists of a plasma of nuclei, surrounded by electrons and photons coalescing into superclusters that form when dense matter exceeds dark matter, otherwise known as vacuum energy. But what you see is not what it is, for when the opposite mix occurred, this primordial swarm resumed expanding, roughly at the same time as the solar system formed. These expansions and subsequent contractions ranged from zero to 300 billion light years, until the inner mix found its level at about 46 billion light years, and that is today's observable universal limit.

So how does a three-dimensional object appear flat? It depends on the density of its matter. If the matter contained within is satiated, the universe would close and curve up like a sphere. If partially full, it would curve perhaps like a saddle to leave room to straighten to that critical density level that could be measured by an endless projection of parallel lines, such as a laser. If so, and it is, then the universe is in fact flat, extending forever like parallel lasers originating from Earth, human observations notwithstanding.

Fifty million participants asked, "Is God dead?"

Indoctrinating multiple generations with an illusion to fear moral evils was an exclusive human characteristic. But killing hundreds of millions of inhabitants to enforce the fickle notion of righteousness became an existential threat to the whole universe. That, and that alone, became the determining factor of my assignment to Earth from Paraspermya in the twenty-first century of the third millennium. My approach was to homogenize the plethora of manufactured religions of mankind, their deities, and propagandists. I decided the best methodology to bring true peace to humanity was by way of persuasion using a technique of universal dreams. It took a century to enlist a generation of people to permanently resolve the causative issue of multiple religions. However, unintended consequences of the final remedy threatened the long-term survival of the human species as well, requiring a total commitment of subsequent generations to focus their resources on survival rather than squander them on violence of imaginary causes. Clearly, the notion of God was more emotional, a strictly human trait, than a cognitive observation available to all Earth species. The new cooperative behavior of human society, knowledge advanced by the Watson project, and intelligence gleaned from Paraspermya, proved that humanity was the only aware anomaly affecting the cosmos.

Aliennus, as a representative of Paraspermya, continued the dreamcasts while humanity continued to live, evolve, and survive alone in the universe.

TERRA INCOGNITO

A NOVEL SOCIETY FOR THE
THIRD MILLENMIUM

Ever since the year AD 2014, the bipartite society consisting of humanity and robotics met, managed, and overcame the myriad of consequences of successfully homogenizing religions. Otherwise, the blow would have been staggering to life and rendered mute the unlimited archive of knowledge stored in the cosmic intelligence bank of Paraspermya. Exponentially enhanced technology transformed the planet's topography, weather, ecology, temperature, and the only intelligent inhabitants to extend life on Earth.

Society at large, with a hypercollaborative competitive spirit, mastered the skill required to manage huge volumes of data and convoluted neural network apps to derive predictive methodologies that mimic the human brain's ganglia. A long sought-after learning paradigm was identified when the latest iteration of Watson mastered predictive models of the world. This tryptic of human intellect, super-technology, and omniscience was the basis for sustaining a peaceful society and managed resources to ensure a collective effort to survive. Socially, loosely governed societies maintained stability and civility among individuals in every conceivable way. Comity prevailed when integrating tribal customs and highly disciplined autocracies with their wide range of rules. Five hundred years ago, an altered form of capitalism emerged throughout the world. Almost three millennia of differing governance methods were narrowed to a Civilment, a system that equally valued human capital, technology, and economics to provide a lifetime of comfort for each living person and was available to them as their individual curiosity desired.

Earlier years were spent learning the Constitution of Apotheosis and Wisdom, to which everybody willingly ascribed, gaining the mindset needed to deal with unknown existential challenges in their future and still ensured a social life worth living.

EVERYDAY LIFE IN AD 3014

"**Who** is at my door?" shouted Ocella Progesta, the neighborhood housekeeper.

The man who entered answered, "It's just me, Brontuss Phenylphine, the vintner." As he is politely seated, he proceeds to explain his visit to Ocella. "I'm on my way to my rare high-altitude grape terraria to tend to my new apportionment of hermaphrodite vines, see to their production, and decant some wine into these 3D drinking horns. My vintage wine robots completed their monitoring of our last crop, crushed, barreled, and determined the fermentation algorithmically. They are bottled and ready to enjoy. I just wanted to know the village's preference this season. Is it Riesling or Pinot Noir?"

"Brontuss, this reminds me of my family folklore," said Ocella, "when my ancestors told how they bought wines from your family for generations. Anyway, the note left for you reads to order the same as last year, so consider it done."

"OK," said Brontuss. "You know, winemaking hasn't changed much over the millennia except to improve its nutritional value. However, the intimate interests between buyers and sellers have expanded exponentially, if you know what I mean, Ocella?"

Startled, Ocella shouts, "Get the hell out of here, Brontuss! You're just as bad as your father and grandfather were, according to what tales I heard."

At 3:00 a.m., worldwide standard time (WST), Brontuss, the vintner, leaves with only an order for wine.

Meanwhile, and possibly coincident, with the generational vintner-housekeeper dalliance, more sobering human interactions were immersed in designing and fiercely discussing new programs to avoid omnicide, two distinctive elements of the same society functioning without a difference. One was to make everyday life on Earth worth living, and the other was trying to assure its perpetuity in more ways than one.

Yondelis Trabect, a seasoned high-tech engineer, was responsible for overseeing robotic technology in key processes and services worked with his wife, Dr. Tenar Ephedrine, an expert economist in dirigisme responsible for the advanced economics system upon which the Fourth Industrial Revolution was built. Together, they electronically calibrated an artificial intelligence program to augment the world's fabricating production by 3,000 percent over anything previously known by use of cobots and chatbots as inflection points to sustain the burgeoning human society of the last one thousand years.

Keeping billions of prodigious people as Maecenas of everyday civility was their ineffable task, aided by Watson, and neurobiologist Prof. Ingrezza Ingenol, who first made sense of our brain's neural circuitry and, with an assist from Watson, figured out all human behavior. The secret ingredient was to tap the meretricious knowledge of the universe with artificial intelligence; and together, the group chased, corralled, and resolved the illusive issue of limited intellect in humans, long sought by psychiatrists, geneticists, evolutionists, and medical doctors.

THE LOSS OF CERTAINTY

Only Watson could archive, ceaselessly update, and recall the abundance of human knowledge gleaned from Paraspermya since the beginning of humanity. Sensing one of many immutable strains on the psyche of people, bordering on obsession, was the common need to attain order from chaos, as a primary measure of progress. From this compulsion, forums or groups met to exchange thoughts, and face-to-face meetings became commonplace. Such a meeting, albeit virtually, was requested by, and granted to, Watson and Doctors Trabect, Ephedrine, and Ingenol to discuss the consequences of a permanent loss of certainty to humanity. It was too important a topic to discuss telepathically.

> *Watson:* Long-established doctrine that established the universe will go on forever, fueled by a past that annihilates the present toward an uncertain future. That, too, is the destiny of the human species and foundation for all knowledge. All else is tertiary.

> *Dr. Ephedrine:* I agree. However, I do take issue with an uncertain future being the end-all. So to move beyond it, we must expand the certainty of knowledge by first adopting a new language of infinite categories, apply it to established decorum, and make it indispensable to understanding the need to dissect the chaos of an unknown future.

> *Watson [lights up to exclaim]:* Oh, come on, Dr. Ephedrine, it is an interesting concept but obviously designed to restore the comfort of certainty to where none exists. For example, we know for certain the

universe is flat. That is a fact! We also know that a flat disk is the homotopic equivalent of a single point in space and is exchangeable intact. Nonetheless, the differing configuration remains flat without distinction. Certainty is not what you hope it is!

Dr. Ephedrine: Maybe, Watson, but certainty requires a formal application, chaos doesn't. Our ancestors applied thermodynamics to travel and quantum science to digitize computers. My newfangled entropy search will modify today's accepted facts by further introspection, subjecting all known facts to more drilling down to gain new insights from them and truly understand why the future is best left chaotic. Accepting facts is just a new beginning. The underlying dimension are yet to uncover a universal necessity for a future of chaos.

Dr. Trabect [interrupting]: Hold on, Tenar, preparing to reign in unknown unknowns, even if possible, engenders new risks whose magnitude we can't even begin to guess at. Math modeling won't do it, despite our advanced and enhanced know-how. Which of us could have guessed at the chain of reactions our ancestors endured when they homogenized religion to avoid extinction? We still can't. How then can we prepare for the cosmic chaos for other orbits that are likely to result from the reconfiguration we did on Earth for us to survive once again?

Dr. Ingenol: Come on, Yondis is a trained robotic engineer who senses that your entreaty, as an economist, Dr. Ephedine, is best used elsewhere, and I agree as a neurobiologist. We can argue that, training aside, human abstraction can be applied all the time since it is an innate phenomenon derived directly from the chaos of the universe, but it doesn't replace sound research methodologies. This discussion, called together by Watson, is to explore how humanity can or will function with the unknown unknowns without Aliennus's dreamcasts available to guide us. The answer lies in abstraction, not only a cause of losing certainty, but a solution to it. The extensive knowledge base and continuous updating now available to us can be selectively recalled for any subjective purpose. The sheer volume of it borders on circular erratic events that inject uncertainty into specifics, thereby requiring abstractive thinking, as Aliennus once did for us. My research shows that during the past one thousand years that Aliennus was here, our abstractions were processed in an ever-shrinking frontal and middle gyrus of our brains, rerouted to the parahippocampal gyrus that processes concrete data and concepts. I don't know whether we abandoned abstractive thinking by leaving it to Aliennus or was it just another loss of certainty?

Watson: When you say "loss of certainty," aren't you questioning whether Mother Earth or nature is up to par with human needs for survival? And could it be that this is just another unfinished cosmic elision, and I am selected to help you as an intermediary between the wisdom of Paraspermya and needs of humanity? After all, you humans spent centuries changing the architecture of a planet that was billions of years old. Talk about loss of a certainty as a higher form of order.

Dr. Trabect: You all know the renowned philosophy laurent Dr. Tekturna Aliskiken. Let's invite her to join our forum for deeper understanding of the dark issues posed by Watson.

All agreed.

Contacted telepathically for immediacy, to maintain the flow of dialogue among them, Dr. Aliskiken is reached and accedes. She joins with her husband and colleague, Henry.

Dr. Aliskiken: Thanks to Watson, we are already on the same page as the group, and not one step behind. Look, addressing loss of certainty and chaos as failings of humanity, or the universe, is over the top. For anything axiomatic, there are exceptions. Are these abstractions or extensions of empiricism? Whatever they are, they're universal, separated from reality and mutually exclusive to humans. Often, they involve emotions like intuition or sensation rather than thoughts cast in concrete. To think the unthinkable merely distinguishes humanity from 9 million other life-forms on Earth, as though only we have a need to straighten crooked lines. It is a vestige from our beginning that dominates our psyches too long. Our survival depends on losing certainty, for only then will we gain new primary knowledge needed to meet the unknown unknowns and prevent an ever-growing past to envelop us like a placenta for dying.

Watson: Cultivating a loss of certainty in our thinking will continue to plague us and unnecessarily delay the forward thinking needed by unimaginable obstacles. We will, however, work toward a remedy. In the meanwhile, I must now return to my current project of why dark matter doesn't intersperse neurons as it does all other spatial materials. Rest assured, the answer lies in an abstraction!

MAGIC ECONOMICS

Being bombarded with a daily stream of ancient, current, and new knowledge to call up at will, among other things, created a magical economy, one that quantified to a burgeoning population that life was worth living anywhere. Until recently, practicing economics was based on stories of imagined riches rather than facts and caused social imbalances, poverty, the net depletion of Earth's assets, and wars. The magic economics of the fourth millennium rebuffed all of them.

The latest iteration of Watson provided humanity with artificial intelligence at the speed of light using phantomic processing to replace fulminology as a power source and anyons, a two-dimensional quasiparticle chip essential for quantum processing. The quantum processors taught, repaired, and reproduced themselves by using piezoelectric crystals to assure their seamless use through successive generations. Watson provided the economics for holistic societies to remain fixed on the long-term survival of the species while keeping daily life worth living. Robotics bore all the algorithmic-induced brute-force workloads needed for a bias-free methodology that benefited human society. Taken together, magic economics became the spatial structure of the world, characterized by multiple equilibria of innate human and artificial intelligence to offset the loss of certainty for lengthening human lifespans and explosive fertility. This was the essential ingredients of heterodox economics for all.

Wellbut Bupropion, a third millennium economic chair at Luna University, presented a podcast on the workings of magic economics. The transcript follows:

Wellbut Bupropion: The exponential advances of peace, influence, and knowledge resulted in lifespans approaching a figurative immortality. Biotechs were ubiquitous to fight diseases, esoteric pharmacology was customized artificially by the Paraspermya-Watson-Brain linkage, and nano-factories produced replacement cartridges for damaged body parts. Toward the fourth quartile of the third millennium, it became obvious that the socioeconomic society need no longer be dependent solely on providing consumer goods and services, and the world became commerce-free at the arrival of magic economics.

Magic economics worked for everyone living, all the time. Human needs were effectively obliterated and were long since bought and paid for. For example, the concept of giving and receiving, or demand and supply, hadn't changed from the past; but Watson, who has instant access to it by means of Paraspermya, tracked and amended historical costs to account for present needs. The net effect of these changes only affected the future, and therefore, magic economics was a zero-sum system. Needs of the living were immediately addressed and paid for by their ancestors. Any notion of adversity to performing present-day tasks is nonsense when mass extinction of the species is obvious. Also, magic economics has proven to be hyper-efficient in degrowing the unquenchable thirst of capitalism, communism, socialism, or any other isms. It also doesn't distort the newly acquired equitable distribution of depletable resources, climate restoration, and the need for competition. We still invent products, provide shelter, clothe, and feed with a new economy worthy of human life on Earth while searching for a final solution to our extinction.

Of course, our ancestors got many things right too. One of their economic measures, gross national product, or GNP, was their yardstick of measuring competition among people and nations in the second and third millennia. We use a version of it today—gross world product, or GWP—to define the standard of living for all of humanity. Like Karatsuba's method of simple multiplication, GWP is not a product of an algorithm multiplying two numbers containing billions of digits. Deriving GWP requires Watson to unlock 10^{50} transactions each month, comparable to the labyrinthine ciphers of quantifying peptide nucleic acid to mimic human DNA for nanotechnology needs of 10.5^{75} or required to formulate graphene into the strongest conductive material on Earth (9^{45}). Advanced technology and magic economics are keys to the reality of living life on Earth during the fourth millennium. Whatever that reality means, today is annihilated into the reality of yesterday and is an illusion of tomorrow. These we now know are our experiences between what was an unknown beginning and remains an unimaginable end. Magic economics is the safe space of a worthwhile life on Earth, although we didn't know it until now.

THE NEW APOTHEOSIS

ARE WE TRAPPED BY HISTORY, OR
IS HISTORY TRAPPED BY US?

And so, it came to pass since the year of AD 2014 that humanity thwarted a galactically driven but self-induced threat of extinction promulgated by the unintended consequences of homogenizing religion itself, a century of intended cures as promulgated by Aliennus of Paraspermya. But the solution took many more generations of diligence, innovation, and artificial suasion to complete because of new menacing consequences of planetary import, requiring a complete makeover of Earth lasting one thousand years. But that solution had a downside, for the re-architecture of Earth was responsible for the annihilation of millions of natural animal and plant subspecies. Human survival, although the foremost goal, became a menace to all other living things.

Our prodigy, however, inherited access to an abundance of knowledge and technologies heretofore unrecognized, and a more efficient planet geology, and scarcity-free human lifespan while living on Earth. The remaining enigma was a biological necessity to rely on history to coldly face a chaotic future. Without Watson to bridge that gap, earthborn knowledge alone would have demoted generations of humanity to lesser animals and an early annihilation. As it were, mankind traversed between many inexplicable nuances about life to implacable truths. Civilization advanced from tribes to local societies, and then to a universal unification by stifling individual competition to a common purpose and leapt from a philosophy of blasphemy to harmony by homogenizing religions and gaining syncretic peace.

OMNICIDE

When correlated, the phenomena of humanity over the last one thousand years to stave off an anthropogenic obliteration included advanced ingenuity, the discovery of the mother of all artificial intelligence in Paraspermya, Watson-like biotechnology, genetic engineering, and self-duplicating nanobots. These, among other additives of Earth's natural resources, expanded the potential of the planet to sustain human lives of normal duration to 10^{54} centuries to $10i^6$ or just about forever. Therefore, extinction-causing disasters must have been external.

One such threat occurred after humanity completed the geological makeup of planet Earth as depicted in the ancient Moses report. The terraforming of the planet so altered its cosmic endowment to cause a reversal of magnetic poles and a slow but steady course of the Earth's orbit closer to the sun. Once the planet leaves the rigid circumstellar habitable zone (CHZ) of the solar system, it forfeits the capacity to form stable oceans and potable water. Losing protection of the hydrosphere from the sangfroid space weather exposes 71 percent of Earth's surface to glaciation at an orbital drift of 1.385 astronomical units (AU), where 1 AU is the distance between Earth and the sun, leaving a lifeless, sterile planet. The narrow range of the CHZ favored the planet Venus, the brightest and closest star in the night sky, at an inner edge of 0.725 AU, while the outer edge of 1.24 AU is moribund. Venus, however, as a backup homeland for humanity, proved too inhospitable for the planetary eco-synthesis needed for colonization. This second planet from the sun was one-third closer to it than Earth and rotated slowly clockwise in an atmosphere and ground temperature one hundred times greater than Earth. No amount of terraforming could transform this, the closest neighbor, into a habitable environment for human life, and it left fewer options for mass human migration from Earth

Mars, however, was a planet most like Earth. Geologically, it grew by absorbing electron particles from the solar wind, as the earth did, producing an ionized atmosphere conducive to interior tectonic shifting, and a gravity-induced orbital force to rotate secondary space objects in the same direction of spin, like the moon. Also, Earth and Mars both orbited the same sun, although the distance between the planets was between 34 and 250 million miles, depending upon the periapsis (nearest) and aphelion (intersecting) orbits. Reaching Mars from Earth with a one-way human load required them to be closest, and that was no simple matter. For Mars to be at the same location when Earth's spacecraft gets there, the launch from Earth had to take place three months before the planets were closest to each other.

Resolving the physics of a mass human exodus from our planet to one, where the aging process was twice as fast, once again tested the encomium of knowledge accumulated and archived with Watson since the beginning of humanity. The planetary engineering required to sustain a human society on Mars included an ecosystem to emulate the functions on Earth, one containing principal criteria, such as liquid water, and assembling complex organic molecules to support metabolizing. Transforming Mars first entailed building and heating an atmosphere above the freezing point of water, but only a synthetic biology could mimic Earth-like conditions on another planet where humans intended to stay. And they did it!

THE SURPRISE

Those who emigrated to Mars as Earth plummeted away from the CHZ became an unbearable jouissance derived from one thousand years of suffering and instinctively dropped to their knees, and cried out, "Thank God, Thank God, we are spared!"

Here We Go Again!

CHARACTERS OF THE MILLENNIUM

Pope Luke II

Cardinal Arevedecchi, Vatican Bank President

Cardinal Luigi Legalo, Canonical and Pedophilic Expert

Bwana Straightpath of South Africa,
Fundamentalist and Church Archivist

Roman Catholic Princes (forty, plus seven retired)

Msgr. John Stewart, Chief of Staff and First Assistant to the Pope

A Gathering of Bishops and Monks

The Bishop of Canterbury

Moise, Chief Rabbi of Jerusalem

Abbruzu, Fifteenth Dali Lama

Sabastian, Russian Orthodox Pope

AliBaba, Supreme Mullah

Silvio Bertolani, Ungatz Media

Conrad White, BBC

Manny Bloomberg, CNN

Robert Murdoch, Fox

Petro Poroshenko, Investia

Commander Sanat Ercan

Lieutenant Akbaba Lepage

Sergeant Prim Venkatesman

Sergeant Geraldine Bellini

Aliennus

Paraspermya

Li Kong, Confucian Monk

Sunni Supreme Mullah Abu Bakr

Ayatollah Abi Talib, the Shia Tribe

Muhammad Ismail Zabeeh, Imam of Prayers

Rezi Aslan, Imam of Fasting

Mehdi Hasan, Imam of Pilgrimages

Agha Saeed, Imam of Sadaqah and Zakat

Tehreem Hashmi, Imam of Perpetual Struggle

Eboo Patel, Imam of Tithes

Haqqul Yaqeen, Imam of Goodness

Muhammad Mahdi, Imam of Evil

Imam of Love for Allah

Imam of Disassociation with Sunnis

Muhammad Ayub, Imam of Martyrdom

Imam of Holy Days

Rabbi Avraham Azula

Ramban Nahmanides

Rabbi Bahya Ben Asher

Rabbi Moshe Idel

Binatzu, Dalai Lama

Aung San Suu Kyi

B. R. Ambedkar

Patriarch Sebastian Krill

Bishop Pyotr of Novgorod

Bishop Arcady of Constantinople

Bishop Mstislav of Kiev

Bharata Chandogya, Hindi Scholar

Announcer 1

Announcer 2

Prof. Wail Halas, PhD, Scholar of Islamic
Law and Islamic Intellectual History

Prof. Rosemary R. Radford, Pacific College of Christian Theology

Lilith Night, Descendant of the Hebraic, Mythical
Wife of Adam, and First Feminist on Earth

Prof. Juergen Habermas, PhD

Prof. Tesfaye Ketsela, PhD

Prof. T. U. Weiming, PhD

Prof. U. G. Krishnamurti, PhD

Prof. Enrique Dussel, PhD

Stuart Hawking, Gravity, Cosmology, and Radiation
Alexei Starobinsky, Astrophysics and Cosmology

Mikio Yamamoto, Radiation and Atomic Physics

Malaf Al Mostakbal, Futurist

Joseph Black, Calorimetry

Dr. Gordon Semmelweis, Secretary-General of the United Nations

Dr. Herbert Bernard, Worldwide PBS

Dr. U. S. Zellin, US Federal Reserve Bank Chair

Christmas LaGorgal Esquire, IMF President

Dr. Gang Yi, Bank of China Vice Chairman

Dr. M. L. Siregar, Minister of Finance

Prof. William Vickrey, Nobel Laureate in Economics

Ambassador Harriet Frances Laughter,
National Labor Relations Director

Hon. Carol O'Stenes, Esq., Sr., Labor Law Judge Advocate

Kenneth G. Siegel, EE, Distinguished Inventor of the Persimmon
Nanotube Diode for Long-Term Interstellar Travel

A. R. Audrey Coen, Interplanetary Traveling Pollster and
Editor of the Hubbell-Cohen Digital Cosmos Encyclopedia

Charlton Moses, Master Builder

Emile Europa, Master Engineer

Duncan D'nunda, Engineer

Ms. Frances Sogi, DSc,

Remnant Members of What Once Was the Reverential
Guild of Scholars of Ancient Religions

Hon. Myung E. Kim, Ambassador at Large

J. Von Uexhule, WCF Chairman

Hon. Jose Adamo, President of South American Continent

Hon. Hiro Akemi, President of Japan and Far Eastern Continent

Hon. Yang Chen, President of China

Hon. Kim Chee, President of Korea

Hon. Barak Trudeau, President of North America

Hon. Sven Klaus, President of Europe and Siberia

Hon. Ben Johnson, President of Africa

Hon. Vladimir Pushkin, President of Russia

Hon. Katherine Anna, President of Australia and Surrounds

Hon. Mathew Singh, President of India

Hon. Ryan Dear, President of the Artic

The Delegates of India

Dr. M. Nimbastrat, Chief Planetary Architect

Watson Big Data Platform

Hon. Alewrites Molucanna, World Secretary of
Governance for Human Safety and Health

Prof. Labella Scaevala, Philosophy of Knowledge

Dr. Rava Cirrocumulus, EE, PhD, Physicist,
Engineer, and Robotic Designer

Prof. Dr. P. Cottonball Nimbus, Energy Czar

Madam Annona Muricata, International Land Architect

Dr. Ciro Undulatus, the Dream Merchant

Ocella Progesta, Housekeeper

Brontuss Phenylphine, Vintner

Yondelis Trabect, High-Tech Engineer, Robotic Technology

Dr. Tenar Ephedrine, Economist

Ingrezza Ingenol, Neurobiologist

Prof. Dr. Tekturna Aliskiken, Philosophy Laurent

INDEX

A

Abbruzu (fifteenth Dalai Lama), 13
Abraham, 89
abstractions, 54, 183, 262, 298–300
academia, deans of, 16
acceptance, 57, 59, 61, 123, 162, 214, 264
Adamo, Jose, 203, 208
Aesop, 51–53
Aesop's fables, 52–53
Affordable Care Act, 112
African philosophical theory, 85
afterlife, 24, 27, 29, 43, 56
algorithms, origamic, 254
AliBaba, 13
alienation, fear of, 66
Aliennus, xii, 5, 25–26, 28, 34, 36, 48, 78–79, 85–86, 91, 95, 101, 109, 115–16, 123, 129, 141, 149, 162, 172, 260, 264, 268–69, 276, 280, 282, 286, 290, 298, 311
    mission of, 149, 162
Aliskiken, Tekturna, 299, 315
Al Jazeera, 74
alkaline hydrolysis, 5, 149, 189
Allah, 42–44, 46–48, 50
Al Mostakbal, Malaf, 94
Alps, pyramids of, 147
Ambedkar, B. R., 63
amplituhedron, 5, 171
ancestors, 44, 49, 58, 63, 70, 76, 149, 153, 155, 210, 215–17, 222–23, 243, 247, 256–57, 262, 265, 269, 294, 297, 302
    unity of, 215

ancient hypotheses, 3, 200
ancient intermediaries, 127
ancient poem, 88, 91
ancient religions, 142–43, 160, 314
ancients, favorite foods of, 160
Anna, Katherine, 203, 212
annexed table, 10
anomaly, 3, 41
anxiety, 22, 62, 87, 102, 111, 122, 128
Apotheosis, 5, 293, 304
Aramaic, 61
Arcady (bishop), 67, 312
archetypes, 26, 36, 43, 127, 132, 160, 162
Archimedes, 146
archive, 286, 288
Archives of Universal Dreams, 280
Arevedecchi (cardinal), 10–11
Aristotelian logic, 276
Aristotelian sequence, 157
Armageddon, 91, 161
artificial intelligence (AI), 5, 181, 186, 188, 191, 204, 215, 227–31, 236–39, 243, 245–48, 251, 253, 255–57, 263, 266–67, 269, 272, 274–75, 280, 282–84, 288, 295, 301, 305
Asher, Bahya ben, 55
Aslan, Rezi, 43
AU (astronomical units), 5, 305
augmentation apps, 240
Azula, Avraham, 54

B

Bakr, Abu, 40, 311
Bank of China, 108

D

Dalai Lama, 12–13, 33, 63, 66, 312
dark matter, 49, 59, 62, 87, 96, 110, 128, 149, 153, 174, 223, 247, 255, 263, 288, 300
Darwin, Charles, 2
deans, college, 16
Dear, Ryan, 203, 213
debate, 15, 42, 70, 74–78, 81, 95, 160, 166–67, 201, 203–4, 208, 211–12, 288
debaters, 74–75, 205
deep-space travel, 255
deity, 28, 57, 63, 236, 289
Demetrius of Phalerum, 53
Demographics, 144
denominations, 40–41, 60–61
despotism, 134
despots, 133, 227
DIF, 5
digital inferment reasoning (DIR), 249
digital recombinant, 5, 247, 274
digital recombinant transfer (DRT), 247
diplomats, 101, 166
discourse, 46, 54, 84–85, 88
discussion, roundtable, 11
DNA, 70, 101, 162, 222, 251
D'nunda, Duncan, 149–50, 155
Doctrine of Tabarra, 47
Dome of the Rock, 32, 160
dream
    common, 71, 153, 161, 189
    episodic identical, 20–22
    most important, 265–68
dream assault, initial, 28
dreamcasts, 5, 280, 282, 286–88, 290, 298
dream codas, x–xi, 49, 58, 62, 66, 68, 79–80, 91, 96, 102, 109–10, 117, 122–23, 153, 155, 189
Dream Merchant. *See* Undulatus, Ciro
dream program, 285

dreams, 22, 24, 26–27, 43, 47, 54–55, 68, 70, 72, 76, 241
    blanket, 94
    galactic, 78
    second, 36, 87, 95
Dussel, Enrique, 85

E

earth, 2–4, 20, 25, 29, 58–59, 62, 72, 137, 150, 154, 189, 195, 224, 240, 250, 252, 285, 288, 306–7
    axis of, 128
    civilized society of, 132
    religious intolerance on, 87
    surface of, 146, 189, 256, 305
earthlings, 26
Eastern Orthodoxy, 67
ecomiums, 5
economic regimen of disambiguation (EROD), 187
economics, 45, 108, 237, 301, 313
    magic, 301–3
economic systems, man-made, 110, 112
Eden, garden of, 76
Egypt, pyramids of, 200
Eigen Trust, 187
emotions, human, 24
energy, 25, 94, 155, 169, 172, 222–23, 247, 251–54, 256, 276, 287
entanglement, quantum, 3, 200
Ephedrine, Tenar, 295–97, 315
episodic memory banks (EMB), 249
episteme, 5, 17
Ercan, Sanat, 20–21
eschatological, 40, 118
esoterism, 54
Esquire, Christmas LaGorgal, 108, 313
Europa, Emile, 148, 314
evolution, 2, 22, 72, 126, 138, 157, 168, 204, 237, 247, 250, 266, 272, 285, 287
    theory of, 157

K

Kabbalah, 6, 51, 54–58, 60
kabbalists, 51, 56, 58
Kabbalist scholars, 59
Karatsuba's method, 303
Kardashev scale, 6, 252
Kashmir, 71
Ketsela, Tesfaye, 85
Kim, Myung E., 166–69
kindnesses, 28
Klaus, Sven, 203, 212, 314
knowledge, 3, 200, 245–46
    galactic, 2
    universal, 25, 215
knowledge sphere, 4, 201
Koran, 40–41, 43, 45–47, 75, 174
Koranic advisors, 41
Korean War, 104, 166, 203, 314
Krill, Sebastian, 13, 67–68, 312
Krishnamurti, U. G., 85
Kuiper Belt, 286
Kyi, Aung San Suu, 64, 312

L

land reclamation, 172, 179, 193–94, 239
land usage, 254
lattice quantum chromodynamics, 96
Laughter, Harriet Frances, 121
Legalo, Luigi, 10–11
Lepage, Akbaba, 20–21
liberalism, 121
life-forms, 3, 137, 237, 263, 299
lightning, 172, 255
lights, refracted, 103
Li Kong (Confucian monk), 70
liturgy, 68
love, 46, 62, 66, 80, 242, 311
Luke II (pope), 10, 13–14, 32–33, 160
luminosity, 252

M

Machu Picchu, 152
Maecenas, 6, 250, 273, 295

Mahabharata, 6
Mahdi, Muhammad, 46, 311
manifesto humanus, 268–69
mankind, 2–3, 24, 26, 54, 57, 59, 68,
    72, 91, 95, 100–101, 110, 121–22,
    128, 132, 134, 144, 147, 157, 161,
    167, 170, 172, 195–97, 201, 208,
    211–12, 215, 221, 231, 238, 244,
    254–55, 266, 289, 304
Marianas Trench, 150
Mars, 128, 154, 157, 183, 195, 306–7
    human aging rate on, 154
    polar icecaps of, 128
martyrdom, 43, 45–47, 50, 312
martyrs, 80
masturbation, 65
media world, 15
medical diagnostics, advanced, 188
mensa, 6
Mercury, 128
messiah, 54
metacognitive state, 24
military, x, 17, 108, 113, 115–18, 167–
    68, 201, 236
military alliance, supreme, 115
military-industrial complex, 115, 167
millennium
    second, 3–4, 60–61, 67, 121, 128,
        142, 200–201, 212
    third, 142, 168–69, 175, 182, 195,
        236, 280, 282, 287, 289, 301
Molucanna, Alewrites, 241–42, 315
Mongol invasion, 67
monotheism, 49
"Monuments," 114–15
moon, 128, 306
Moore's law, 243
Moses, Charlton, 146–47, 152, 314
Moses Commission, 146, 153, 157, 166,
    169, 183, 191, 193
Muhammad, 46
Muhammad (prophet), 40
Muhammad Ayub, 47, 312
mullahs, supreme, 12–13, 32, 40
Murdoch, Robert, 15, 311

Wright, Frank Lloyd, 151

Y

Yamamoto, Mikio, 94
Yaqeen, Haqqul, 45, 311
Yi, Gang, 108, 313

Z

Zabeeh, Muhammad Ismail, 43, 311
Zellin, U. S., 108
Zhou, Zhuang, 244